Old English Preverbal *Ge-*: Its Meaning

Matth. VIII.

> do he ssund up dat vormullet
> worde dat ghesproken was
> dor den propheten ysaiam de
> dar sprak he hefft uns be-
> nomen vnde vnse wedage
> hefft he gedragen. Do dat
> ihc sach vele schare vmme siik
> hees do het he he gan ouer
> dat mer. Do gink to em en
> schriuer vnd sprak meyster
> ik wil di volgen tho wor du
> gheyst do sede em i. de vosse
> hebbet ere hol vn de voghe-
> le des hemels ere neste
> mer des mynschen sone ne
> hefft nicht dar he zin ho-
> uet to noghe. Vn en and'
> sprak to eme en va zinen
> iungeren he' lat my aller-
> erst gan vn begraue my-
> ne vader do sprak i'c to em
> volghe my lat de doden be-
> grauen ere doden

MS Thott 8, 8° showing *benomen*, corresponding to Northumbrian *genom* in the OE text (Matt. 8:17), and *to noghe*, corresponding to West Saxon *ahylde* and Northumbrian *gebeges* (Matt. 8:20). Courtesy, Royal Library, Copenhagen.

Old English Preverbal *Ge*-: Its Meaning

J. W. Richard Lindemann
Virginia Polytechnic Institute and State University

The University Press of Virginia
Charlottesville

THE UNIVERSITY PRESS OF VIRGINIA
Copyright © 1970 by the Rector and Visitors
of the University of Virginia

First published 1970

Standard Book Number:
Cloth, 8139-0319-x; Paper, 8139-0320-3
Library of Congress Catalog Card Number: 79-130689
Printed in the United States of America

To the Memory
of
Le Baron Russell Briggs
and
George Lyman Kittredge
in Gratitude

Preface

ANY attempt to clarify the nature of so controversial a morpheme as Old English preverbal *ge-* necessarily involved two problems: first whether or not the prevailing doctrine insisting that the morpheme was a marker of aspect was tenable; second, if not tenable, whether or not one might explain the morpheme by trying to ascertain its original lexical meaning. These two problems are separately treated in Part I and Part II respectively.

Inasmuch as the discussion of the problem presented in Part I was the most urgent of the two, was, as Roger Lass puts it, a "clearing of the ground,"[1] it was submitted for publication as a separate article in the *Journal of English and Germanic Philology*[2] long before the research for Part II was completed. But Part I was composed in anticipation of Part II even then, is essentially a prolegomenon to it, and is consequently here combined with it.

In a preliminary consideration of the two problems it became immediately clear that much would depend upon the nature of the corpus that was to furnish the data upon which any ultimate interpretations of the morpheme must rest. It had to be representative of the speech current at the time the document was written; it had to be a translation, for only then would it be possible to effect the beginning of correlating an unknown linguistic unit with one that was known; it had to be composed of several texts in different Old English dialects translating one and the same Latin text. And it had to be sustained prose. The only work readily available that presented a corpus that would respond to all of the above demands was Skeat's edition of the chief Old English dialect translations of the Gospel of Saint Matthew. The dialect versions were collated with their Latin sources; dialect was collated with dialect; Latin source was collated with Latin source. Finally, in order to increase the mass of correspondences, the frequencies of situations providing context of *intent*, and in general to increase the inventory of linguistic facts supporting the predictability of the lexical meaning of the morpheme, the six collations mentioned above were again collated with texts of Matthew in some of the other older Germanic dialects.

My debt to others is great. I wish to thank the Board of Editors of the *Journal of English and Germanic Philology* for their permission to reprint my

---

[1] Roger Lass, *Approaches to English Historical Linguistics* (New York, 1969), p. 249.
[2] "Old English Preverbal *Ge-*: A Re-examination of Some Current Doctrines," *JEGP*, LXIV (1965), 65-84.

article here as Part I and the librarians of Det Kongelige Bibliotek in Copenhagen for their permission to quote from MS Thott 8, 8° and to reproduce the page used here as the frontispiece. To Professor Robert West, of the University of Georgia, I am deeply indebted for his having relieved me of many duties in order that I might have the time to pursue my research; to Professors Calvin Brown and William Free, of the University of Georgia, Professor Hans Käsmann, of the University of Heidelberg, Professor Robert Kellogg, of the University of Virginia, and Professor Norman Eliason, of the University of North Carolina, for having read and evaluated the manuscript for Part II. To Professor Sherman Kuhn, of the University of Michigan, I must express my sincerest gratitude for his words of sustaining encouragement during many years of research. And, finally, I must acknowledge my great indebtedness to the liberality of the Research Division of the Virginia Polytechnic Institute and State University for material aid, without which the publication of this work might have been considerably delayed.

J.W.R.L.

Blacksburg, Virginia
May 1970

Contents

Preface	vii
Abbreviations	x
Part I: A Re-examination of Some Current Doctrines	1
Part II: The "Meaning" of the Morpheme: Empirical Assumptions and Linguistic Evidence	19
Works Consulted	67

Abbreviations

IE.	Indo-European	L.	Lindisfarne MS
PGmc.	Proto-Germanic	O.	Alfred's *Orosius*
Goth.	Gothic	M.	Monsee Fragments
OE.	Old English	T.	Old High German *Tatian*
ME.	Middle English	K.	Middle Low German Bible
NE.	Modern English	Th.	Quatuor Evangeliorum versio Saxonica
OHG.	Old High German		
NHG.	Modern High German	I.	Icelandic New Testament
MLG.	Middle Low German	G.	*Die gotische Bibel*
NLG.	Modern Low German	Wyc.	Wycliffite Bible
Lat.	Latin	Rh.	Rheims Version
C.	Corpus MS	A.V.	Authorized Version
R.	Rushworth MS		

Old English Preverbal *Ge-*: Its Meaning

Part I
A Re-examination of Some Current Doctrines

DESPITE an occasional statement to the contrary, Anglo-Saxonists in general are agreed that the many attempts to determine the meaning and the function of the OE preverb *ge-* have been unsuccessful or, at best, badly confused. During the last century and a half there have appeared some thirty-five dissertations, monographs, and articles—to say nothing of a host of glossarial commentaries—that purport to explain this morpheme and its cognates but fail ultimately to do so. As recently as 1953 Professor Herbert Pilch of the University of Kiel, attempting to account for the disappearance of the morpheme in ME, was compelled to admit that "über ae. ʒe- herrscht noch immer weitgehende Unklarheit."[1]

Obviously there must be some reason for this frankly admitted obscurity, and the reason appears to be twofold. In the first place the preverb *ge-* has a very high degree of relative frequency. We know that in any spoken language a linguistic element with a high degree of relative frequency demands less emphasis than an element that appears more rarely and, consequently, may lose a specific denotation and acquire a very general one or several less specific and very general ones. We know that this happened with the OE preverbs *ā-*, *be-*, and *for-*, and there is no reason for assuming that this should not have happened with *ge-*.

But a more important and immediate reason for the obscurity, I believe, lies in the nature of the very doctrines that have been proposed to explain the morpheme. In too many instances these have been accepted as infallible articles of faith presumably founded on incontrovertible facts. Yet when they are subjected to close critical scrutiny they leave the impression that they are, after all, only primary assumptions not yet able to sustain themselves by means of adequate proof, or they appear to be philosophical hypotheses rather than strictly linguistic observations confined to a homogeneous language *system*. At times these doctrines reveal a very seductive cogency, but only in the light of data that have been especially selected to substantiate them; when they are more generally applied to different sets of data, they are likely to collapse. Moreover, too frequently they substitute questionable syntactic assumptions for "jene semasiologischen untersuchungen" that Hans Pollak recognized as the only proper approach to an ultimate understanding of the

[1] Herbert Pilch, "Das AE. Präverb ʒe," *Anglia*, LXXI (1953), 129.

meaning and function of such a preverb as *ge-*.[2] But above all, these doctrines place too much reliance upon evidence produced by a comparison of a Germanic text with its Latin or Greek source alone, despite the fact that experience has taught us that translators and glossators at best follow their sources only capriciously. Not a single one of the doctrines proposed in the essays mentioned above supplements the evidence from the single source by drawing upon the equally illuminating evidence that could be derived from a comparison of one Germanic dialect with another.

Unfortunately many of the doctrines continue to thrive in the authoritative sanctity of classrooms, of grammars, and of textual notes. If they thereby perpetuate the obscurity surrounding the preverb, then they ought to be questioned, for the prominence of the preverb is such that it cries out for resolute endeavor on our part to understand it—even if our initial efforts lead us no further than understanding what it does *not* mean. With its high degree of frequency we may safely assume that the preverb *ge-* was an important thread in the whole fabric of OE, and we may also consequently assume that without a clearer understanding of it we miss many shades of meaning originally intended to be expressed in our texts, and we may even risk mistranslating those texts grossly. The fact that the doctrines apparently do not clarify the significance of the preverb suggests that these doctrines require re-examination.

It is my purpose in this paper to make such a re-examination. Most of the doctrines will be discussed only briefly; the one that is now most current and that insists that *ge-* be involved in the theory of aspect will be discussed in more detail. The doctrines that purport to explain the morpheme I present below, and comment upon them in the light of whatever critical evidence is available, some of it taken from the observations of others, some from my own. Wherever I adduce evidence of my own, this is drawn from a synchronic study composed of three OE dialect versions of the Gospel According to Saint Matthew as edited by Skeat,[3] the corpus netting some nine thousand instances of verbal usage both simplex and compound.

I. *Ge-* Is Without Meaning

This doctrine is still widely held, although it is over two hundred years old. Thomas Benson of Oxford lent it some authority when in his *Vocabularium Anglo-Saxonicum* (1701) he said, "*Ge-* apud Saxones semper fere superfluum." In the eighteenth century Adelung's HG dictionary repeated it and doubtless

---

[2] Hans W. Polak, "Studien zum germanischen Verbum," *PBB (Beiträge z. Geschichte d. deutschen Sprache u. Lit)*, XLIV (1920), 380.

[3] In *The Holy Gospels in Anglo-Saxon, Northumbrian, and Old Mercian Versions* ..., ed. Walter W. Skeat (Cambridge, 1871–87).

gave it considerable popularity.[4] And in our own century, one relatively recent OE grammar[5] says that *ge-* "adds little or nothing," and Professor Samuels[6] of Glasgow and Miss Hollmann[7] of Jena find that in general it is "meaningless." Moreover, this doctrine has had far-reaching consequences; assuming that it was meaningless, *speculation* had somehow or other to account for its existence in the language, and on the basis of such speculations Martens, in 1863, constructed his hypothesis implying that the function of the preverb was the same as that of the preverbs in the Slavic languages and that, having lost all lexical meaning, it served merely as a tag to indicate completed action.[8] Streitberg agreed with him.[9] The notion was pure conjecture.

The chief objection to the doctrine will be apparent at the end of this paper. For the time being, suffice it to say that this assumption overlooks the fact that all too frequently simplex and *ge*-compound have *different meanings* that cannot have developed solely out of the concept of completed action: *gan* means 'to go,' *gegan* may mean 'to go away,' 'to happen,' and also 'to walk,' and *gegan* + acc. normally means 'to conquer'; *standan* means 'to stand' and *gestandan* may mean 'to stand up,' but *gestandan* may also mean 'to stop' *and* 'to *remain* standing.' Moreover, it also overlooks the fact that in OE we have contrasting pairs of compounds each of which has a meaning different from that of the other: "ðonne hæbbe we begen fét *gescode* ... ðonne bið us suiðor oðer fót *unscod*."[10] Finally it ignores the fact that in both the Epinal and Erfurt glosses Lat. simplexes are frequently glossed by OE compounds, not OE simplexes.

II. *Ge-* Stresses or Intensifies the Action of the Verb

As one might suspect, this doctrine is fraught with considerable ambiguity and subjectivity. For what, one may ask, is one to understand by "intensifying the action" of a verb? Is *ge-* presumed to mean the same as OE *swiðe*, 'very much'? What is an "intensified" *going*, or *seeing*, or *standing*? Even Streitberg rejected such an assumption and quite rightly saw the absurdity of the multi-

---

[4] J. C. Adelung, *Grammatisch-Kritisches Wörterbuch der hochdeutschen Mundart* (Leipzig, 1796), s.v. *Ge*.

[5] G. P. Krapp and A. G. Kennedy, *An Anglo-Saxon Reader* (New York, 1929), p. xci.

[6] M. L. Samuels, "The *Ge-* Prefix in the Old English Gloss to the Lindisfarne Gospels," *Transactions of the Philological Society* (London, 1949), p. 66.

[7] Else Hollmann, "Untersuchungen über Aspekt und Aktionsart unter besonderer Berücksichtigung des Altenglischen" (unpubl. diss., Jena, 1936), p. 102.

[8] Heinrich Martens, "Die verba perfecta in der nibelungendichtung," *KZ*, XII (1863), 31–41, 321–35.

[9] Wilhelm Streitberg, "Perfective und imperfective actionsart im Germanischen," *PBB*, xv (1891), 70–178.

[10] *King Alfred's West-Saxon Version of Gregory's Pastoral Care*, ed. Henry Sweet, EETS (London, 1871), p. 45, ll. 12–15.

plicity of meanings that were being attributed to *ge-*: "Was überhaupt die 'intensiv' -bedeutung von *ga-* anlangt," he says, "so ist es damit übel bestellt: überall wo man dies erklärungsmittel anwenden will, gerät man in verlegenheiten.... Wie ist es überhaupt möglich, daß eine einzige partikel *zugleich* so verschiedene functionen wie die genannten in sich vereinige ...?"[11] E. Bernhardt apparently originated this doctrine in 1870,[12] and Lorz repeated it in 1908.[13] It still prevails in some circles,[14] but the writers who apply it do not explain what they mean by it any more satisfactorily then Wackernagel did when he said that *ge-* qualifies the meaning of a verb by being "unübersetzbar leise verstärkend."[15]

III. *Ge-* May Convert an Intransitive Verb into a Resultative Verb That Is Transitive

P. Lenz, in 1886, is the first to have published this observation;[16] Lorz repeated it in 1908 (p. 14), and the doctrine has often been reiterated since. Nevertheless, to be quite exact, as we must be in these matters, the statement is not wholly true, but an inaccurate re-creating of an older syntactical system in the image of a modern one. It is true enough that such compounds as *gegan* and *gesittan* may at times be followed by accusatives, and at other times may not. But when they are followed by accusatives they are not therefore necessarily transitive; rather they can still be intransitive followed by an accusative of direction or goal;[17] e.g., *Beowulf* 2100: "ond he hean ðonan ... meregrund *gefeoll*," 'he fell on to (down to) the bottom of the lake,' not "reached by falling."

IV. *Ge-* Indicates Completion

Although this doctrine may appear to be identical with the one immediately following, which states that the preverb perfectivates, there are a few qualifications inherent in the one or the other that warrant treating them separately. Jacob Grimm was apparently one of the first to observe that the preverb had the power to indicate that the action of the simplex to which it was prefixed was accomplished.[18] Wackernagel stated simply that its function was to

---

[11] Streitberg, *PBB*, xv (1891), 91-93.
[12] E. Bernhardt, "Die Partikel Ga als Hilfsmittel bei der gotischen Conjugation," *ZfdP*, II (1870), 160-62.
[13] Ant. Lorz, *Aktionsarten des Verbums im Beowulf* (diss., Würzburg, 1908), pp. 12-15.
[14] See Bertil Weman, *Old English Semantic Analysis and Theory* (Lund, 1933), *passim*.
[15] Wilhelm Wackernagel, *Altdeutsches Wörterbuch*, 5th ed. (Basel, 1878), s.v. *ge*.
[16] P. Lenz, *Der Syntactische Gebrauch der Partikel "ge" in den Werken Alfreds des Großen* (diss., Darmstadt, 1886), p. 12.
[17] B. Delbrück, *Vergleichende Syntax der indogermanischen Sprachen*, Erster Theil (Straßburg, 1893), p. 365.
[18] Jacob Grimm, *Deutsche Grammatik*, 2nd ed. as revised by Scherer (Berlin, 1878), II, 829.

terminate the concept of the action, "um den Begriff der Thätigkeit abzuschließen" (s.v. *ge*). But observe the astonishing exegesis of some subsequent writers intent on reconciling the idea of completion with the unwarranted assumption that *ge-* must originally have meant 'with, together' and must have been the Germanic equivalent of Lat. *cum*. Dorfeld assumed that the preverb originally meant 'together,' and that this idea of 'being together' indicated completeness, and subsequently indicated completed action.[19] Wustmann understood the evolution of completion somewhat differently: *ge-* originally meant 'with': from this it went into the meaning of 'fully,' entirely,' and then 'entirely to the end.'[20] Van Swaay followed a similar kind of speculative progression: from the idea of "union" could come the idea of "collecting together," and from there on the prefix could indicate a point in the action that would be the equivalent of a "result."[21] If all this strikes the reader as being somewhat complicated, he will simply have to accept it as a matter of record; it was typical of the semasiological gymnastics that were tried in an effort to extract from the idea of 'with' an idea of completion that was not there.

Once this doctrine of completion was established it became extended to syntax, specifically to the tenses. The function of *ge-*, it said, was to indicate completed temporal action and thereby provide verbal compounds that would compensate for those tenses, the equivalents of the Lat. perfect tenses, that never developed in the Germanic languages. Wackernagel claimed that it gave to the preterite the sense of the perfect and the sense of the pluperfect; to the present it gave the sense of the perfect, the future, and the future perfect (s.v. *ge*). Lenz believed that the prefix served to indicate the pluperfect and the future perfect,[22] and even Streitberg believed that, prefixed to a verb in the present tense, it could indicate the future.[23] The doctrine sweeps down into the twentieth century; Bloomfield and Mossé accepted it without question,[24] and Samuels applied it to the Lindisfarne Gospels as late as 1949.[25]

---

[19] Carl Dorfeld, *Über die Function des Präfixes ge-* (*got. ga-*) *in der Composition mit Verben* (diss., Gießen, 1885), p. 45.

[20] Rudolph Wustmann, *Verba Perfectiva namentlich im Heliand* (diss., Leipzig, 1894), pp. 18-23.

[21] H. A. J. van Swaay, *Het prefix ga- gi- ge-, zijn geschiedniss, en zijn invloed op de 'actionsart,' meer bijzonder in hed Oudnederfrankisch en het Oudsaksisch* (Utrecht, 1901), p. 44.

[22] Lenz, *Der Syntactische Gebrauch*, p. 20.

[23] Streitberg, *PBB*, xv (1891), 121-23.

[24] Leonard Bloomfield, "Notes on the Preverb *ge-* in Alfredian English," in *Studies in English Philology: A Miscellany in Honor of Frederick Klaeber*, ed. Kemp Malone and Martin B. Ruud (Minneapolis, 1929), pp. 82, 83, 84, 87, 90, 93, 95, 97, 100, 101; F. Mossé, *Histoire de la forme périphrastique être + participe présent en germanique* (Paris, 1938), II, 9.

[25] Samuels, "The *Ge-* Prefix," pp. 81-90. (But here too, as in the rest of his paper, Samuels has the idea that the use of the prefix is determined by the "length of the Lat. verb"!) See also Karl Dahm, *Der Gebrauch von gi- zur Unterscheidung perfectiver und imperfectiver Aktionsart im Tatian und in Notkers Boethius* (diss., Borna-Leipzig, 1909), pp. 18-30, and Hermann Hirt, *Handbuch des Urgermanischen* (Heidelberg, 1934), III, 126.

Ge- thus presumably functioning to indicate the perfect tenses is known as the "perfectic *ge-*."

The doctrine of the "perfectic *ge-*" was the product of an all-too-hasty generalization. That any completeness expressed by *ge-* had to be a *lexical* completeness, a completeness per se, "in sich selbst," L. Tobler pointed out a century ago.[26] (For example, a verb like NE *upend* is composed of a simplex *end* and a preverb *up-*. The *up-* indicates a local goal and may therefore be regarded as locally limiting or, some would say, completing the action expressed in the simplex. But in such a statement as "He had upended the beam when we got back" the *temporal* completion is obviously not effected by the preverb *up-* but by the grammatical category of the past perfect tense.) Mourek objected to the doctrine of the "perfectic *ge-*" on the same grounds as Tobler,[27] and Behaghel showed that preterite *ge-* compounds in temporal subordinate clauses did not necessarily express a pluperfect sense, because simplexes in that position could be interpreted in the same way.[28] The data from the OE Matthew also disprove the doctrine; they reveal the following low percentages of *ge-* compounds in relation to simplexes:

> *Ge-* preterites translating Lat. perfects   16%
> *Ge-* preterites translating Lat. pluperfects   15%
> *Ge-* present indicatives translating Lat. futures   20%[29]

V. *Ge-* Perfectivates or Expresses Perfective Aspect

The doctrine that *ge-* perfectivates is similar to the previously mentioned doctrine except that the latter is now thrust into a verbal system analogous to that in the Slavic languages and is tricked out in terminology borrowed from Slavic grammar. Reduced to its simplest terms, the doctrine states that in the older Germanic dialects the simple form of the verb, with some very few exceptions, expressed an action in its continuity whereas the compound verb expressed an action that was cut off, or brought to an end, or completed.[30] The doctrine was first proposed by Heinrich Martens.[31]

Streitberg developed Martens' thesis in a long essay on Goth. *ga-*, an essay that was destined to become for many generations the classical *locus criticus* from which to explain the uses of preverbal *ge-* in most of the older Germanic dialects. Borrowing the term *Aktionsart* ("manner of action, character") from

---

[26] L. Tobler, "Über die bedeutung des deutschen ge- vor verben," *KZ*, XIV (1864), 124–33.
[27] V. E. Mourek, reviewing a dissertation by Wustmann, in *AfdA*, XXI (1895), 195ff.
[28] O. Behaghel, *Deutsche Syntax* (Heidelberg, 1924), II, 112.
[29] W. Streitberg, in *Urgermanische Grammatik* (Heidelberg, 1943), p. 280, warned against confusing perfective *Aktionsart* and the perfect tenses. Yet cf. Frank G. Banta, "Tense and Aspect in the Middle High German of Berthold von Regensburg," *JEGP*, LIX (1960), 81–83.
[30] See Streitberg, *Urgermanische Gramm.*, pp. 276–81.
[31] Martens, pp. 329–31.

Delbrück to translate Slavic *vid*, a manner of *regarding* an action, Streitberg insisted that the Germanic languages made the same distinction between imperfectivity and perfectivity that the Slavic languages did. "Die *perfective* actionsart," he said, "fügt dem bedeutungsinhalt, der dem verbum innewohnt, noch den nebenbegriff des vollendet werdens hinzu. Sie bezeichnet also die handlung des verbums nicht schlechthin in ihrem fortgang ... sondern stets im hinblick auf den moment der vollendung."[32] Then, like Martens, he insisted that the original meaning of *ga-* ("mit," "zusammen") had faded out and been *reduced to zero*; consequently, when it was prefixed to a simple verb, it "perfectivated" that verb (enabled it to indicate that the action of that verb was completed) *without modifying the meaning of the verb* (p. 103). Its function, he assumed, was the same as that of *po-* in Slavic.

This doctrine pretty well dominated the first half of the twentieth century and found a somewhat modified expression in Leonard Bloomfield's essay in 1929. From the viewpoint of explaining *ge-* this essay differs very little from Streitberg's as far as fundamental concepts are concerned. Although Bloomfield tried "to illustrate the use of *ge-*" and did so accurately enough in terms of purely descriptive syntax, his discussion was limited to only eight OE verbs —far too few to support any kind of generalization—and he failed to "explain" the prefix. Instead of *Aktionsart* he used the term *aspect* and, like Streitberg, he believed that the situation in OE was like that in Slavic: "As a matter of fact, where OE expresses aspect, it reserves the punctual (verb with prefix) for unit action and classes repeated, habitual, and generalized acts with the durative (uncompounded verb; more explicitly *beon* with present participle), exactly as does Slavic" (p. 92).

All of these doctrines are still current, but it is the last of these, V, that has assumed the most important role in practically all current grammars, textbooks, and dictionaries; for these inform us that *ge-* perfectivates, that it expresses perfective aspect, that its original function was to indicate completion, or that it makes a durative verb "punctual," i.e., causes it to indicate the beginning of an action or the end of it.[33] Despite the skill with which this doctrine is sometimes formulated, the more one works with it and tries to apply it to the older Germanic dialects, whether Old English or Gothic or Old Saxon, the more one realizes that it will not accommodate itself to linguistic facts. And it is this doctrine that demands our closest critical scrutiny.

In practice, the doctrine simply does not work. When Friedrich Weick, a

---

[32] Streitberg, *PBB*, xv, (1891), 71.

[33] See, for example, Karl Brunner, *Altenglische Grammatik nach der angelsächsischen Grammatik von Eduard Sievers* (Halle/Saale, 1951), p. 308, n. I; Randolph Quirk and C. L. Wrenn, *An Old English Grammar* (New York, n.d. but preface dated 1957), pp. 79–80, 110-11; Fernand Mossé, *Manuel de l'anglais du Moyen Âge*, 1, Vieil-anglais (Paris, 1950), 148–50; G. L. Brook, *An Introduction to Old English* (Manchester, 1955), p. 62; Martin Lehnert, *Altenglisches Elementarbuch* (Berlin, 1959), p. 103; Henry Sweet, *Anglo-Saxon Primer*, 9th ed. (Oxford, 1957), p. 40.

disciple of Streitberg, examined the Lindisfarne Gospels, applying Streitberg's hypothesis, he discovered that the forms of the verbs in his text were different from what he believed they ought to be, and he suggested emendations in accordance with his hypothesis.[34] "Das Simplex sollte stehen," he says under *biddan* on page 3, "an Stelle des fälschlich gesetzten Kompos." On page 7, under *hyran*, we find "Das Simplex sollte stehen," "Das Kompos. sollte stehen," and on page 5 we read, "Das Simplex ist einige Male belegt, aber sonderbarerweise immer an unrechter Stelle"![35] But instead of questioning his doctrine, Weick apparently preferred to believe that the glossators of Lindisfarne were unfamiliar with their own language: "Noch deutlicher führen uns die zahlreichen Beispiele, wo geschrieben werden mußte: 'das Simplex oder das Kompositum sollte stehen' vor Augen, wie sehr groß schon die Verwirrung in bezug auf die Anwendung von Simplex und Kompositum war" (p. 49).

Lenz, too, had difficulties, even with the orderly prose of Alfred. Assuming that *ge-* was "syntactic," he encountered instances where the use of *ge-* failed to coincide with the provisions of his theory. Again and again we find observations like "kein grund zu *ge*" (p. 30), "*Ge* ohne grund" (p. 25, 20; p. 38, 104; p. 34, 111, 112; p. 40, 119), and "warum *ge?*" (p. 39, 110; p. 45, VI). H. Hesse, too, had trouble reconciling doctrine with facts.[36] Substituting the doctrine of the *Aktionsarten* for Lenz's "syntactic *ge*" he found many passages that defied his formula, two examples of which will suffice: under *healdan* (p. 17) he says "Besser paßt jedoch das Komp.," and under *leornian* (p. 47) "... doch ist das Komp. ... wohl vorzuziehen." An excellent example of how the doctrine of the *Aktionsarten* in the Streitbergian sense can seduce one into grave mistranslation occurs in Hesse's treatment of a passage on page 25, under *standan*: "Ða ʒestod se byscop æt hire" Hesse translates as "trat an sie heran" but admits that the translation is not exact because the Latin original is durative, "*adstans.*" Nevertheless, he reads 'stepped over to her' because the verb is compounded with *ge-* and must, therefore, according to his doctrine, be "punctual." Thomas Miller's translation in the EETS edition is much nearer the truth: "then the bishop stood by her."

Lorz also found that Streitberg's doctrine was inadequate when applied to certain *ge-* compounds in *Beowulf*, especially when he discussed *beodan* (p. 45), *habban* (p. 54), *stæppan* (p. 65), and *þolian* (p. 68). And Streitberg himself had to admit that his hypothesis could not explain *gahausjandona* (p. 83), *gahauseiþ* (p. 80), *sitands* (p. 87), and *gahabaida* (p. 90); in order to save his doctrine, like Weick, he had to postulate textual corruption.

The whole business of depriving *ge-* of any meaning, of making it a "formal"

---

[34] Friedrich Weick, *Das Aussterben des Präfixes ge- im Englischen* (diss., Darmstadt, 1911).
[35] Weick. See also pp. 11, 12, 15, 17, 19, 21, 22, 23, 25, 27, 29.
[36] H. Hesse, *Perfective und imperfective Aktionsart im Altenglischen* (diss., Münster, 1906).

index of perfective aspect, of "stretching the Germanic languages out on the Procrustean bed of Slavic"—Hirt's phrase—simply has not explained it. Pertinent indeed is Hans Pollak's assertion: "Vertrauenerweckender sind daher jene semasiologischen untersuchungen, die irgend eine vorsilbe als solche gelten lassen und nicht auf das wittern bestimmter actionsarten ausgehen."[37]

Despite the fact that many textbooks still acknowledge Streitberg's thesis, competent Slavicists have long ago annihilated it—as well as his assumption that aspectual situations in the Germanic languages are like those in Slavic.[38] Granted that there are similarities between early Germanic dialects and Slavic, Streitberg's critics pointed out that the verbal *systems* of the two differed greatly.

Briefly this difference is as follows. In Slavic the verbal system is composed of *two sets* of verbs, the verbs of one set being used to indicate that the action of an utterance must be viewed without reference to its completion, the verbs of the other set being used to indicate that the action must be viewed *with* reference to its completion. (This is tantamount to saying that for every Germanic verb, Slavic has two verbs.) One *or* the other of the verbs of these two sets *must* be used in order to indicate whether the action (1) is (was, will be) in a state of happen*ing* (imperfective) or (2) was (will be) in a state of happen*ed* (perfective). This contrast in the duration expressed in the utterance is what is properly called *aspect*. Aspect, then, in Slavic is determined by a *grammatical* category, is mandatory, and is *syntactic*.[39] On the other hand, there is nothing at all like this in the Germanic dialects. In these dialects a preverb may modify the action of a verb in such a manner as to indicate that the action tends toward a local goal, and even sometimes that it reaches such a goal and thereby completes the action per se, e.g., *overdo, undergo, bequeath, bypass*, or *uphold*. Such completion, however, is inherent in the semantic substance of the *word*, part of its essential meaning; completion is here not syntactic but *lexical*. What we have operating here is not aspect but "manner of action," *Aktionsart* in its true sense. *Aktionsart* is objective; aspect is subjective.[40] For an excellent exposition of the distinctions between the situations in the Slavic languages and the Germanic, one must read C. R. Goedsche, "Aspect versus Aktionsart" (*JEGP*, XXXIX[1940], 189-97).

[37] Pollak, *PBB*, XLIV (1920), 380.
[38] See especially the substantial objections expressed by the following: Carl Recha, *Zur Frage über den Ursprung der perfectivierenden Function der Verbalpräfixe* (diss., Dorpat, 1893), pp. 77-79; V. F. Mourek, *AfdA*, XXI (1895), 195 ff.; Antonin Beer, "Beiträge zur gotischen Grammatik," *PBB*, XLIII (1918), 446-69; B. Trnka, "Some Remarks on the Perfective Aspects in Gothic," in *Donum Natalicium Schrijnen* (Nijmegen-Utrecht, n.d.), pp. 496-500.
[39] A. Meillet, *Le slav commun* (Paris, 1924), pp. 240-44; Wenzel Vondrák, *Vergleichende slavische Grammatik*, 2nd ed. (Göttingen, 1928), II, 373 ff.; E. Koschmieder, "Studien zum slavischen Verbalaspekt," in *KZ*, LV (1928), 301.
[40] Horst Renicke, "Die Theorie der Aspekte und Aktionsarten," *PBB*, LXXII (1950), 152-86.

These two terms, *aspect* and *Aktionsart*, have too long been used interchangeably, the resulting confusion having seriously blurred our understanding of the functions of compound verbs. Modern linguistics insists that these two terms and what they stand for must be kept rigorously and distinctly apart.[41] They are so kept apart in the remaining portion of this discussion.

In the article mentioned above, Goedsche insisted that *ge-* could not be a formal index of perfective aspect.[42] In 1953, comparing Biblical passages in OE with identical passages in Russian, Polish, and Serbian, Pilch revealed that the old equation *simplex: ge- compound : : imp. aspect : perf. aspect* no longer holds true.[43] And in 1958, Philip Scherer, using a technique of chrones and chronemes for typical verbal sets, showed that OE *ge-* compounds as such do *not* express aspects: *hælde* and *gehælde* are both perfective and *biddað* and *gebiddað* are both imperfective; "aspectual connotation is not a function of form."[44]

However, Pilch limits his evidence to only a few Biblical passages and their Slavic parallels, and Scherer limits his to verb forms out of context. Both of them cite *only* West Saxon evidence, Scherer erroneously assuming that the West Saxon version is a "translation of the Lindisfarne Gospels." But inasmuch as it is frequently assumed that the function of preverbal *ge-* differed according to the several OE dialects, in what follows below I adduce evidence not only from "classical" OE as well as Alfredian OE but from three of the major dialects also. Moreover, I resort to a simpler and, I believe, clearer method of demonstrating aspectual connotations than those mentioned above; that is, I record complete predications, both independent and dependent, containing *ge-* verbal compounds and test them, first by showing that a certain aspect must follow *logically*, second by subjecting the predications to corollaries inherent in the aspect theory. This method will reveal that *ge-* verbal compounds are not *ipso facto* "perfective" but that they may also just as well be "imperfective" or "durative."

The quotations that follow are from the three dialect versions of Matthew mentioned above and from *King Alfred's Orosius*, ed. Henry Sweet, EETS (London, 1893). C. = Corpus MS (West Saxon), R. = Rushworth MS (Mercian), L. = Lindisfarne MS (Northumbrian); O. = Orosius, Wyc. = Wycliffite translation, Rh. = Rheims translation. The Latin is from the Lindisfarne

---

[41] E. Hermann, "Aspekt und Aktionsart," in *Nachrichten von der Gesellschaft der Wissenschaften zu Göttingen, Philologisch-Historische Klasse aus dem Jahre 1933* (Berlin, 1933), pp. 470-80; Josef Raith, *Untersuchungen zum englischen Aspekt: I. Teil, Grundsätzliches, Altenglisch* (München, 1951), pp. 21-32; Karl Ammer, *Einführung in die Sprachwissenschaft* (Halle, 1958), I, 1967-69.
[42] P. 196.
[43] Pilch, *Anglia*, LXXI (1953), 131-33.
[44] Philip Scherer, "Aspect in the Old English of the Corpus Christi MS.," *Lg.*, XXXIV (1958), 251.

Some Current Doctrines

MS. Wherever I found it pertinent, I have given a generally accepted translation of a *ge-* compound beneath the quotation. The doctrine correlating *ge-* with the aspect theory and the corollaries inherent in it are considered in the following examples.

I. "When OE expresses aspect it reserves the punctual (verb with prefix [ge-]*) for unit action* ['complexive,' 'perfective' action] *and classes repeated, habitual, and generalized acts with the durative (uncompounded verb)."*

It is true that according to the theories of aspect a perfective verb is always punctual.[45] But is a verb compounded with *ge-* punctual? The various doctrines that we have examined earlier in this paper consistently assumed that it was, but the quotations that follow, both those from Matthew and those from Orosius, when subjected to tests inherent in the theory of aspect, show that *ge-* compounds are not necessarily punctual but often durative.[46]

1. The context may indicate the durativity:

Matt. 12:46
    C.   þa stod his moder 7 his gebroðra þær-úta
    L.   Heonu moder his 7 broðero stondas ł *gestodon*
             ecce mater eius et fratres stabant foris
    Lenz   (p. 48), "bestehen"
    Lorz   (p. 36), "beistehen"
    Hesse   (p. 25), "persistere"
    Wyc.   "stoden without forth"
Therefore, not 'stopped' but 'continued to stand'

Matt. 13:2
    C.   and eall seo mænigeo stod on þæm waroþe
    L.   and all ðreat *gestod* on wearðe
           et omnis turba stabat in litore
    Cf.   MHG *gestân* in *Das Nibelungenlied* (ed. Karl Bartsch [Leipzig, 1931]), stanzas 136, 4; 460, 3; 864, 4, where it is durative and means 'to remain standing' 'to live.' Note that the Lat. of both passages is in the imperfect tense.

Matt. 2:23
    C.   he com þa 7 eardode on þære ceastre
    L.   cuom *gebyde* in ceastra
           ueniens habitauit in ciuitate

---

[45] See Hirt, *Handbuch*, III, 130, and Behaghel, *Deutsche Syntax*, II, 95.
[46] Van Swaay, *Het prefix ga- gi- ge-*, found nineteen *ge-* compounds in OS that were durative. His explanation of the durativity on the grounds that the meaning of a compound can undergo a shift ("kan een verschuiving ondergaan") is forced.

Not 'took up his residence' or 'established himself' or 'settled,' but 'abode' there
Hesse (p. 15), "verbleiben"
Wuth (p. 62), "verharren, verweilen"[47]

Matt. 5:5
L. eadge biðon ða milde forðon ða agnegað eorðo
R. ... þa milde forþon þe hie *gesittaþ* eorðu
Beati mites quoniam ipsi posidebunt terram
Not 'will take into their possession' but 'will own' it: = NHG *besitzen*

O. 276, 1. þæt he his rise ... mid micelre unieðnesse *gehæfde*.
Not 'had had' but 'preserved, retained, held'
Hesse (p. 39), "bewahren"

II. A truly punctual verb cannot express the present tense; only the past, future, and future perfect.[48] However, *ge-* verbal compounds *do* express true present tense:

Matt. 6:2
C. swa liceteras doð on gesomnuncgum
L. Suæ legeres *gewyrcas* in somnungum
sicut hipocritae faciunt in synagogis
Lenz (p. 40), "ausrichten"
This passage nicely illustrates the difference between *Aktionsart* and aspect. If Lenz is right, as I believe he is, then *gewyrcas* indicates terminative *Aktionsart* (indicating a goal), but the entire utterance, even though the action were construed as iterative, would still be imperfective. Note also that here a "repeated, habitual, and generalized" act is expressed by a *compounded* verb, *not* by an "uncompounded" one.

Matt 7:14
C. hu neara ... is ... se weg þe to life *gelædt*
R. *læde*
L. *lædes*
quam angusta ... uia quae ducit ad uitam
Hesse (p. 37), "fortführen"
Here again the compounded verb, *not* the uncompounded, expresses an "habitual and generalized" act: The way leads on to life now and always. Note again terminative *Aktionsart* but imperfective aspect.

---

[47] Alfred Wuth, *Aktionsarten der Verba bei Cynewulf* (diss., Weida i. Thür., 1915).
[48] See Hirt, *Handbuch*, III, 130; Streitberg, *PBB*, xv (1891), 75, 120-24; Meillet, *Le slav commun*, pp. 242-44; Ammer, *Einführung*, pp. 167-69.

Some Current Doctrines

Matt. 6:7
- C.   þonne ge eow *gebiddon*. nelle ge sprecan fela
- L.   ðonne gie *gebiddas* nallas ge felo ... gespreca
-    Orantes autem nolite multum loqui
- Wyc.   "in preiynge nyle ȝe speke moche"
- Rh.   "vvhen you are praying"

Matt. 18:26
- C.   Hlaford *gehafa* geþyld on me
- R.   haefe
- L.   haefe
-    patientiam habe in me
- Lenz   (p. 56), "festhalten"
- Clark Hall–Meritt (p. 164), "hold, preserve."[49] Not a punctual 'have,' but 'continue to have patience with me'

Matt. 5:4
- C.   Eadige synt þa þe nu wepað
- L.   eadge biðon ða ðe *gemænas* nu
-    Beati qui lugunt
- Lenz   (p. 61), "beklagen"
- Wyc.   "Blessed be they that moornen"

Note that the addition of *nu* stresses the idea of the present. The weeping is "in der erlebten Zeit als verlaufender Prozess dargestellt";[50] 'who are in the process of mourning *now*.'

III. Since a perfective (punctual) verb can have no true present, it cannot have a present participle.[51] But verbs compounded with *ge-* appear again and again in present-participial form:

Matt. 20:20
- C.   com to him ... modor mid hyre bearnum hig *ge-eadmende*
-    accesit ad eum mater ... cum filliis suis adorans
- Rh.   "the mother ... vvith her sonnes, adoring"
- Wyc.   "with her sones, onourynge"

Matt. 26:27
- L.   *genimende* calic ðoncunco dyde
-    accipiens calicem gratias egit

---

[49] John R. Clark Hall, *A Concise Anglo-Saxon Dictionary*, 4th ed., with a supplement by Herbert D. Merritt (Cambridge, 1960), s.v. *habban*.

[50] Ammer, p. 167.

[51] Meillet, p. 242: "De même, le participe présent, qui indique d'ordinaire un procès simultané à un autre, ne se prête pas à l'aspect perfectif et il n'y a de participe présent que dans le verbe imperfectif."

      Lorz   (p. 77), "an sich nehmen"
      Wuth   (p. 44), "annahm"
      Rh.   "And taking the chalice"

Matt. 25:31
      C.   þa mænegu wundredon *geseonde* ... blinde *geseonde*
             turbae mirarentur uidentes ... caecos uidentes
      Wyc.   "the puple wondride: seyinge ... blynde men seyinge"

Matt. 13:48
      C.   saeton be þam strande þa gecuron hig þa godan
      R.   bi waraðe *gesittende* gecuron þa gode
             secus litus sedentes elegerunt bonos
      Rh.   "sitting by the shore, they chose out the good."

O. 110, 10: nu ic wille eac þæs maran Alexandres *gemunende beon* (i.e., 'be remembering')
      Lenz   (p. 61), "sich errinnern"
      Lorz   (p. 59), "sich errinnern"

IV. Only durative actions admit of modifiers expressing an extent of time;[52] *punctual actions do not.* The following passages, however, reveal that OE *ge-* verbal compounds not only were modified by expressions indicating an extent of time but also that they themselves indicated a duration of time *during which* another action proceeds simultaneously:

1. General extent of time:

Matt. 2:9
      L.   heno steorra ... fore-*geeade* hea wið þ ... gestod
                       ... antecedebat eos usque ... staret
      Wyc.   "went befor hem, til it ... stood"

Matt. 13:30
      L.   forletas egðer ... *gewæxe* wið *to* hripe
             sinite utraque crescere usque ad messem
      Wyc.   "suffre ȝe hem bothe wexe in to repynge tyme" (i.e., 'continue to grow')

Matt. 19:20
      R.   eall ic þaes *geheold fram* iuguðe mine
      C.   *geheold*
      L.   *geheold*
             omnia haec custodiui
      Lorz   (p. 20), "erhalten, bewahren"
      Wuth   (p. 81), "erhalten"

[52] Hirt, *Handbuch*, III, 130; Hermann, "Aspekt und Aktionsart," p. 478.

Some Current Doctrines

O. 185, 15. si þþan he *gefor* ofer þa monegan þeod *oþ* he com to Alpis
This is the syntactic pattern which, according to Mossé, established his *durée limitée* for the periphrastic form. "Il exprime qu'une action a duré jusqu'à un certain point.... C'est donc avec *oþ*, *oþþæt* que l'on rencontre ce tour" (*Histoire*, I, 86).

O. 72, 26. Ac hine Gandes seo (ea) þaes oferfæreldes *longe gelette* ('hindered him for a long time').
    Lenz   (p. 47), "verhindern"
    Wuth   (p. 88), "aufhalten"

2. *Specific extent of time*:

Matt. 9:20
    L.   heonu wif ðiu blodes flouing *geðolade ł gedrog tuelf uinter*.
        ecce mulier quae sanguinis fluxum patiebatur duodecim annis

Matt. 4:2
    L.   mið ðy *gefaeste feuortig daga*
        Cum ieiunasset quadraginta diebus
Not a *hapax legomenon*, nor, despite the Latin, is there any compulsion to translate this as 'when he *had* fasted'; cf. Matt. 6:16, "miððy ... gie gefæstas (cum ieiunatis)" and Matt. 9:15, gefæsdon (ieiunabam)."

O. 182, 19. Ahsige þonne eft *hu longe* sio sibbe *gestode*: þonne waes þaet *an gear*
    Lorz   (p. 37), "stehen bleiben"
    Hesse   (p. 25), "perstare"
    Lenz   (p. 48), "bestehen"

O. 254, 6. siþþan *gestod* Romeburg XII winter ... *þa hwile* þe Augustus þa eoðmetta wiþ God *geheold*

O. 78, 32. he digellice ... *v gear* scipa worhte and fultum *gegaderode*
Here *gegaderode* is just as durative as *worhte*; *v gear* modifies both.

3. *Time during which other action proceeds simultaneously*—"genuine durative actions ... i.e., those where the segment of time occupied is viewed as a possible container of other acts" (Bloomfield, p. 92):

Matt. 6:7
    C.   þonne ge eow *gebiddon*, nelle ge sprecan fela
    L.   *gebiddas*
    R.   *gebiddandæ*
        orantes autem nollite multum loqui
    Wyc.   "in praying"

Matt. 17:5
- R. þende he þa *gespræc* henu wolken liht oferscuade hie
at huc eo loquente ecce nubis lucida obumbrauit eos
- Wuth (p. 20), "aussprechen"
- Wyc. "ʒhit the while he spake"
- Rh. "as he was yet speaking"

Matt. 13:25
- L. mið ðy uutodlice *geslepdon* ... ða menn cuom fiond his
cum autem dormirent homines uenit inimicus eius
- Rh. "But vvhen men vvere a sleepe, his enemy came."
Notice, not 'fell asleep' or 'when they had slept' (both punctual) but 'while they were sleeping.'

Matt. 27:32
- L. mið ðy *geeadon* ... gemoeton monno cyriniscne
Exeuntes ... inuenerunt hominem cyreneum
Not 'after they went out' or 'when they *had* gone out' but 'as they went out'
- Wyc. "and as thei ʒeden out"
- Rh. "and in going"

The passages cited above amply illustrate the proposition that *ge-* compounds do not necessarily determine perfective aspect, that they may, just as readily, determine imperfective (or durative) aspect. Jacob Grimm had observed this twofold characteristic of the compounds long ago,[53] causing one to wonder all the more why just this one morpheme, *ge-*, should have been singled out from among the whole group of inseparable prefixes—all of which *may* at times "perfectivate"—as a distinctive and exclusive marker of perfective aspect.

Mutatis mutandis the simplexes, too, fail to support the current doctrines. They are not necessarily durative. Here, again, *aspect depends upon context*, and, as the following passages clearly reveal, simplexes may stand in utterances that are indubitably perfective:

Matt. 1:25
- C. Heo *cende* hyre ... sunu
- R. gebær
- L. gecende
  peperit

---

[53] Grimm, *Grammatik*, II, 821.

Some Current Doctrines

Matt. 4:7
    C.   ne *costna* þu drihten
    R.   *costa*
    L.   *costa*
          temtabis

Mat. 17:6
    C.   hig *feollon* on hyre ansyne
    R.   *feollan*
    L.   *gefeallon*
          ceciderunt

Not 'were falling on their face' but, Wyc., "feldon doun on her face" —a sudden "unit" action

Matt. 13:31
    C.   gelic senepes corne þ*seow* se man on hys æcre
    R.   *seow*
    L.   *geseow*
          seminauit

Again "unit action." But note the following, where the aspect is imperfective:

Matt. 13:4
    C.   þa þa he *seow*. sume hig feollon wiþ weg
    R.   *seow*
    L.   *saues*
          seminat

These above two passages, with their similiarty of *form* clearly reveal the extent to which aspect in OE is subjective, syntactic, and, with the exception of the "expanded form," *entirely dependent on context*.

Matt. 28:2
    C.   drihtnes engel ... awylte þone stan 7 *sæt* þær on uppan
    R.   *gesett*
    L.   *gesæt*

Not 'was sitting on' but 'seated himself.' Cf. *Beow.* 490: "site nu to symle."

Wyc. "turned awey the stoon, and sat thereon."

Now, if OE simplexes, as we have just seen, are capable of expressing *perfective* aspect as well as imperfective, and if *ge-* compounds are capable of expressing *imperfective* aspect as well as perfective, then *ge-* cannot be a "formal," preverbal tag indicating perfective aspect. We find for OE what

Scherer[54] found for Goth. and OHG, namely, that *form*—always excepting the expanded form—does not determine aspect, but that aspect is a *connotation* inherent in specific verbal meaning *and* syntactic context. *Ge-* has no immediate bearing on aspect at all, and the doctrine is untenable.

We return for a moment to Streitberg. Streitberg, "empruntant malheureusement la terminologie des langues slaves" (Mossé, *Histoire*, II, 2), appears to have been correct in his statement about the preverb only if we accept it with the following reservations: (1) that the verbal system of the Germanic languages was not like that of Slavic; (2) that the preverb could not have been reduced to zero semantically; (3) that the compounds produced by this preverb *ge-* did not express "perfective aspect" but *might* express a terminating *Aktionsart* as we understand it today. But even this *Aktionsart* would have to be regarded as a secondary signification of *ge-*. Its primary signification would have had to be its *lexical meaning*, for, regardless of the time at which it became and remained a productive morpheme, a preverb expresses an *Aktionsart*, "perfectivates" if you will, only by virtue of its lexical meaning,[55] "indem es ein bestimmtes Ziel seines Simplex scharf betonte."[56] That such meaning was 'with, together' is most doubtful; the ideas inherent in *with*, *together* do not "perfectivate" or terminate.[57]

That *ge-* had lexical meaning is practically certain (Grimm, Grassmann, Pott, and Sievers all believed that it had), and it devolves upon historical linguistics to *abstract that meaning from within* the system of the Germanic dialects. "Streitberg möchte zwar perfektivierendes und lokales *ga-* durch eine unüberbrückbare Kluft trennen: die Sprachgeschichte aber verlangt ihre Vereinigung."[58]

---

[54] Philip Scherer, "Aspect in Gothic," *Lg.*, XXX (1954), 223; "Aspect in the Old High German of Tatian," *Lg.*, XXXII (1956), 424, 434.
[55] Behaghel, II, 96.
[56] Lorz, p. 14.
[57] Behaghel, II, 97.
[58] Wustmann, p. 20.

Part II

The "Meaning" of the Morpheme: Empirical Assumptions and Linguistic Evidence

Denk nicht. Schau.
WITTGENSTEIN

IN Part I of this discussion we saw that the linguistic evidence that we examined simply did not support the current doctrines purporting to explain the meaning or the function of the OE preverbal morpheme *ge-* or, for that matter, any of the other Germanic reflexes of PGmc. **ga-*; and that consequently, despite the grammars and the handbooks, these reflexes of **ga-* were not markers of perfective *aspect* or markers of "punctual acts." The widely spread assumption that they were is due to an inordinate, romantic preoccupation on the part of some scholars of the Germanic dialects with the Slavic dialects, plus a generous amount of what Hjelmslev was wont to refer to as "transcendental linguistics"—the substitution of pure speculation for the laborious, objective examination of a prefix per se, which Pollack had recommended long ago.[1] Moreover, as André Joly has observed, the assumption was one that had been too hastily conceived.[2]

The need for abandoning these current doctrines—especially the insistence that the morpheme is a marker of aspect or that it makes an intransitive verb transitive—is becoming more and more obvious to men devoted to precise examination of the older Germanic dialects. This need is certainly implied in André Joly's article; and it is made practically mandatory in a study by the Russian scholar L. S. Limar, whose investigation of *Beowulf* appeared in the same year that Part I of this essay was submitted to the press and whose conclusions were identical with those of Part I.[3] Limar's study is penetrating and thorough, and because his observations are those of one whose native language makes him especially sensitive to aspectual distinctions it is fitting that they be given here in some detail.

First of all, Limar points out that there are no purely aspectual prefixes *even in the Slavic languages,* and that perfectivation is a phenomenon of a *semantic*

---

[1] Hans W. Pollak, "Studien zum germanischen Verbum," *PBB*, XLIV (1920), 380.

[2] André Joly, "*Ge-* préfixe lexical en vieil anglais," *Canadian Journal of Linguistics,* XII (1967), 78–79.

[3] "K voprosu o roli glagol'nix pristavok v svjazi s vidovym značeniem glagolov (na materiale drevneanglijskogo)," *Učenye Zapiski,* XXVIII, Č. 2-ja (Moscow, 1963), 159–74. I am very much indebted to Professor M. M. Makovskij in Moscow for having furnished me with a copy of this article.

nature (pp. 159-61). "In languages where the aspectual differences are not part of the very *form* of the verb the decisive influence of context and, in particular, of adverbs on the aspectual meaning of the given verb is frequently encountered. This is precisely the condition which we find in Old English" (p. 165). "In Old English 'essentially there was no form for the imperfective aspect,' and since there was no imperfective aspect, that is, one of a correlative pair was absent, there obviously could be no system of aspects, since the system is built on correlatives" (p. 160). Turning to his own corpus he continues as follows: "In the Old English texts which we studied ... we found a large number of examples of the use of simple verbs in contexts demanding the meaning of perfective aspect, and prefixed verbs in contexts demanding the meaning of imperfective aspect" (p. 162)—the very opposite of what was claimed by the older hypothesis.

As examples of *simplexes* in contexts demanding the meaning of *perfective* aspect Limar cites the following from *Beowulf*: 55, "fæder ellor *hwearf*"; 108, "þæs þe he Abel *slog*"; 1281, "siþ þan inne *fealh* Grendles modor"; 1392, "no he on holm *losaþ*"; 1477, "gif ic æt þearfe þinre scolde aldre *linnan*"; 1960, "þonnon Eomor *woc* hæleþum to helpe." And as examples of *ge-* compounds in contexts requiring the meaning of *imperfective* aspects he cites the following: 175, "Hwilum hi *geheton* æt hærgtrafum"; 290, "Ic þæt *gehyre* þæt þis is hold weorod"; 910, "þæt þæt ðeodnes bearn *geþeon* scolde ... folc *gehealdan*"; 1359, "ðær fyrgenstream under næssa genipu niþer *gewiteð*." "All in all, we found in the text of *Beowulf* 70 instances of the use of the simple verbs in a context demanding the meaning of a perfective verb and about 50 instances of the use of prefixed verbs in a context demanding the meaning of an imperfective verb" (pp. 162-64).

Limar concludes his discussion with some remarks on *ge-* + past participle. It has long been known that in the earlier stages of the Germanic dialects the past participle regularly appeared without the prefix, but Limar throws additional light on it in relation to the question of perfectivity: "as analysis shows, there are in Old English a rather large number of participles *without prefixes* in situations demanding a *perfective aspect: Beowulf*, 307, hy sæl *timbred* ... ongyton mihton; 405, byrne scan, searonet *seowed*; 917, Ða wæs morgenleoht *scofen* ond *scynded*; 1192, Him w s ful *boren*; 1124, wæs hira blæd *scacen*.... At the same time the *prefixed* participle II can be used in situations demanding the meaning of an *imperfective* aspect: *Beowulf*, 1884, Ða wæs on gange gifu Hroðgares oft geæhted; 1957, forðam Offa wæs geofum ond guðum ... wide *geweorðod*" (pp. 170-71).

For our purpose here the following observations by Limar are most pertinent: "There can be only one conclusion drawn from these data: Old English verbs, alone, taken out of context and not connected to any particular adverbs, can *not* be recognized as particular aspectual forms.... *Neither can the verbal prefixes be in any way considered aspectual determinants*" (p. 166, italics mine).

Had Limar worked with an OE corpus other than *Beowulf* he might have disposed of another questionable Streitbergian assumption—the assumption that the perfectivating function of *ga-* was proved by the fact that in Gothic *duginnan* is never followed by a *ga-* compound.[4] This holds true enough for those texts that we have in Gothic, but when we turn to Old English, the assumption breaks down. For in the OE Gospels there is ample evidence to show that *onginnan was* followed by *ge-*compounds. I cite only a few:

L. Matt. 11:7, ongann *gecuoeða*; Matt. 11:1, ongunnun *genioma*; Mark 5:18, ongann *gebidda*; Luke 14:30, ongann *getimbra*
C. Luke 19:37, ongunnon *geblissian*; Mark 13:4, onnginnað beon *geendud* (!)[5]

In the light of the above discussion, it would perhaps be better apropos the *ge-* compounds not to use the term *perfectivation* at all.

In the most recent of the essays to appear on our morpheme, a study of Gothic *ga-* undertaken at the University of Paris, Maurice Marache comes to conclusions little different from those mentioned above—without revealing *why* the morpheme functions as it does.[6] He does, however, pull it out of its involvement with aspect and prepares the way that will enable us to proceed to a rational solution of our problem. In agreement with other scholars, he asserts that an aspectual marker indicates a grammatical category; it expresses the attitude of a speaker or beholder and is subjective; a marker of an *Aktionsart*, however, involves a *semantic* unit, and what it expresses is inherent in a lexical unit and is consequently objective. As Marache states it, the *Aktionsart* "erscheint in lexicalischen Gegensätzen, wie z.b. in den paaren *venir—arriver*, *wachen—erwachen*" (p. 5). Simplex and compound then are contrasting *lexical* units, two entirely different words.

Consequently in the context of our problem and the attempted solution of it a preverb even in order to mark an *Aktionsart*, imperfective or perfective, *must have* lexical meaning. But to say that OE *ge-* expresses an *Aktionsart* is not enough—all preverbs are capable of expressing some one of the *Aktionsarten*, at times even a terminative *Aktionsart*. And here most of the critiques of our morpheme rest. But to try to explain the function of a preverb by constantly

---

[4] *PBB*, xv, 109. Cf. Otto Behaghel, *Deutsche Syntax* (Heidelberg, 1924, II, 113.

[5] The source of my own data and the point of departure of this whole study was a collation of three OE dialects as found in Walter W. Skeat, *The Gospel According to Saint Matthew in Anglo-Saxon, Northumbrian, and Old Mercian Versions, Synoptically Arranged, with Collations Exhibiting All the Readings of All the MSS* (Cambridge, 1887). Matthew was chosen because it represented a linguistic document not only presumably idiomatic but also free of the conventions of poetry and the only sustained document, even Biblical, that contained the three dialects West-Saxon, Northumbrian, and Mercian. The Latin source is usually that of Lindisfarne, but collated with that of Rushworth and with Royal MS I. B. XII, the MS that most nearly approaches the one presumably used for the Corpus translation.

[6] Maurice Marache, "Die gotischen verbalen *ga-* Komposita im Lichte einer neuen Kategorie der Aktionsart," *Zeitschrift für deutsches Altertum und deutsche Literatur*, XC (1960-61), 1-36.

dwelling upon its *Aktionsart* is futile, for an *Aktionsart* is merely a secondary characteristic, a by-product of the action expressed by a verb; it is not a *significant feature* distinguishing it from other preverbs, and even if it is known that a preverb perfectivates, such knowledge will not reveal the meaning of the compound of which it is a part. Therefore, to distinguish the preverb *ge-* from other preverbs in Old English, and to explain its function, it is first necessary to try to determine its lexical meaning, for, as Wustmann's observation at the close of Part I indicates, its power to perfectivate must be reconciled with its "local" meaning.

I

"Zusammen"

When I say that it is first necessary to determine the lexical meaning of the preverb *ge-*, I undoubtedly imply that I question the second basic principle of Streitberg's hypothesis, namely, that Goth. *ga-* (or any other reflex of PGmc. **ga-*) corresponded to "IE *co-*" and meant "zusammen," and that it "perfectivated" because its "material" content had been reduced almost or fully to zero.

There are many contradictions in this observation of Streitberg's. Let us first examine the assumption that the lexical meaning of the reflexes of PGmc. **ga-* had been reduced to zero. This assumption did not originate with Streitberg; it was inherited from the eighteenth century, when Benson, in 1701, asserted that "*ge-* apud Saxones" was "semper fere superfluum,"[7] and when Adelung in 1796 repeated it. Samuels and Hollmann insist upon it even to this day. A full-fledged disciple of Streitberg has to assert that the morpheme was *completely* reduced to zero. Otherwise it would not be grammatical and could not therefore express perfective aspect. Consequently Mossè's remark: "Pour que l'aspect soit exprimé de façon absolument nette, il faut que des préverbs se vident de tout sens concret pour être réduits au rôle d'instruments grammaticaux, de morphemes de l'aspect."[8] If the preverb fails to lose its concrete meaning *completely* "l'aspect reste en germanique quelque chose d'accessoire" (p. 2), and this is precisely what those who champion the idea that *ge-* is a marker of aspect cannot afford to admit. For as soon as such a prefix reveals that it has meaning, the theory of aspect flies out the window. Streitberg could not insist too strongly on absolute zero, for there were four verbs in Gothic that he could not accommodate to his hypothesis: *gagaggan, galisan, garinnan, gahaitan*. In these verbs, he said, *ga-* had to mean "zusammen" (*PBB*, xv, 102).

---

[7] Thomas Benson, *Vocabularium Anglo-Saxonicum, Lexico Gul. Somneri Magna Parte auctius* (Oxford, 1701), s.v. *ge-*.

[8] Fernand Mossé, *Histoire de la forme périphrastique être + participe présent en germanique* (Paris, 1938), II, 2.

But to assume that the reflexes of *ga- were without concrete meaning runs contrary to logic and empirical evidence. These reflexes were, after all, members of a large linguistic class, the class of the preverb, every other member of which is known to have had lexical meaning. They form a *system*. To deny one unit of the *system*—the one which in all the dialects had the highest frequency of occurrence—any meaning at all is due either to caprice or the chagrin resulting from inadequate research. It is a well-known fact that a linguistic system will not tolerate the luxury of a useless member; "Die Sprache ist allem Luxus abhold." Some kind of meaning it must have— phonemic, morphemic, or syntactic. "Die Annahme dass der Begriff der Perfectivität aus der Bedeutung der Partikel herzuleiten sei," wrote Wilmanns, "lehnt Streitberg wohl mit Unrecht ab."[9] That the morpheme *ge*- had meaning is simply beyond all doubt. Empirical evidence for it abounds; even the mere context of utterances will show that *gegan* is different from *gan*, *gefaran* from *faran*, *gedon* from *don*, provided that we remember Wilmann's observation that the preverb was in many instances not mandatory. These differences exist even without invoking a distinction in the *Aktionsarten*. And they *still* exist even when the *Aktionsarten* are alike, as illustrated by the following contrasting pairs:

Matt. 16:19. Swa hwæt swa þu ofer eorþan *ge*binst ... swa hwæt swa þu *un*bindest

Matt. 27:31. *on*geredon hine ðy ryfte 7 *ge*geredon hine mið his gewedum

Our immediate concern is not so much with whether or not the morpheme had meaning as with the question of whether or not that meaning was 'zusammen.'

In insisting that the reflexes of PGmc. *ga- meant 'zusammen' Streitberg was expressing agreement with two of his contemporaries: "Die erklärer, vorab Bernhardt und im anschluss an ihm Dorfeld ... gehen von der grundbedeutung des *ga*- = idg. *co-* 'zusammen' aus.... Wol ist 'zusammen' die grundbedeutung von *ga*-, aber diese ist auf der uns vorliegenden stufe des gotischen sprachlebens bei weitaus den meisten fällen in der verbalcomposition geschwunden, oder doch abgeblasst" (*PBB*, xv, 102). But here again Streitberg is not quite accurate. Dorfeld does not correlate *ga*- with IE *ko; he correlates it with Lat. *com-*, which, in general, is one of the morphemes with which our reflexes of *ga- do correspond. But most of the other writers who discuss these reflexes correlate them with Lat. *cum* and insist that these reflexes meant 'zusammen, mit' or, as every English dictionary that I have consulted puts it, under the lemma *y-*, "together." And it is this definition of the meaning of the morpheme that has prevailed in articles, handbooks, and dictionaries for over three hundred years. For as early as 1659 William Somner, discussing "Ge apud Saxones," says that "in compositione idem

---

[9] W. Wilmanns, *Deutsche Grammatik*, II (Strassburg, 1922), 169 Anm.

quandoque valet quod *cum* Latinis."[10] It is this correlation, this assumption that *ge-* is equivalent to Lat. *cum* and means 'together' or 'with' that constitutes the very nucleus of our problem and obstructs our understanding the morpheme, both as to meaning and as to function.

The above correlation and meaning both appear to be wrong; they encounter too many logical and linguistic objections. And inasmuch as these objections provide the very motive and justification for this paper, they must be presented in considerable detail as follows:

1. In the first place it is extremely difficult to find any surviving contexts, especially in Old English, in which *ge-* as a preverb can be translated as "together' or 'with' and still make sense in the utterance. I can recall none. Usually when the Anglo-Saxon writer wishes to express the idea of 'together' or 'with' he does so in precisely these terms:

Matt. 15:32. C. *togædre* geclypedum; R. *to-somne* cliopade
      10:1. C. *to-somne* gecigdum; R. *to-somne* cegende
      27:62. C. comon *togædre*
Mark 14:31. C. *mid* þe to sweltene; R. swelte *mið* ðe

The situation in Gothic is the same:

Mark 12:28, *samana* sokjandans; Mark 8:11, *miþ*-sokjan; 2 Cor. 12:18, *miþ*-insandian; 2 Cor. 8:18, gaþ- an-*miþ*-sandidum

It is interesting to note that in the glossary to his *Gotische Bibel*, when he defines *ga-* compounds, Streitberg translates the *ga-* of his lemmata with "zusammen" only four times and with "mit" only once—despite his hypothesis. And in three instances in Mark where Streitberg translates *ganiman* with "nam *mit* sich," Luther translates the Greek source of *ganiman* with "nam *zu* sich."

2. Second, during all of the three hundred years that have been devoted to discussions of the morpheme no one has ever proved that *ge-* or any of its cognates meant 'with,' 'together."' Evidence for it is absolutely nil. The *only* thing in the nature of evidence that these discussions propose is the observation that in a substantial number of instances *ge-* compounds translate Lat. compounds in *com-*. This is not conclusive evidence for two reasons: first, because Lat. compounds in *com-* are frequently translated by OE compounds in other prefixes also (*a-*, *be-*, *of-*, and *to-*), and in the Anglo-Saxon Gospels *ge-* compounds correspond to Lat. compounds in *com-* no more than they do to compounds in *ad-*. The comparative, quantitative distribution in the three dialect versions of Matthew respectively is as follows:

	C.	R.	L.
ad-	46.1%	42.3%	61.5%
com-	37.1%	42.8%	62.8%

[10] William Somner, *Dictionarium Saxonico-Latino-Anglicum* (Oxford, 1659), s.v. *ge-*.

These figures represent correspondences of *lexical units*, and it is interesting to note that in C. correspondences in *ad-* are even 10 percent higher than those in *com-*. The second reason why the correspondence of *ge-* compounds with Lat. compounds in *com-* does not prove that *ge-* meant 'with,' 'together' is that *com-* itself originally did not mean 'with' or 'together,' as we shall see in more detail later. What is important at the moment is that in the light of the above statistics *ge-* cannot be regarded as the exclusive semantic equivalent of *com-*; it can just as well be regarded as the equivalent of *ad-*.

3. There is a third objection. If *ge-* meant 'with,' 'together,' the verbs to which it was affixed could not be "perfective" or, as Mossé prefers to call them, "determinative." *With, together*, indicate a *rest* relation, and, in the terminology of logic, a relation that is "symmetrical" (↔). In order to be "perfective" or "determinative" a preverbal morpheme must indicate or imply movement from one point to another, one situation to another, or indicate direction forward in space on to a goal; it must express a relation which in terms of logic is "intransitive—asymmetrical" (→).[11] As Behaghel expressed it more than forty years ago "soweit Präfixe perfektivieren, tun sie dies in folge ihrer *räumlichen* Grundbedeutung. Und zwar sind es insbesondere Präfixe, die den *Übergang aus* einem Berührungszustand *in* einem Nichtberührungszustand oder das Umgekehrte bezeichnen" (italics mine).[12]

4 The fourth objection is a purely historical and practical one, for the meanings 'with,' 'together' confronted so competent a historical linguist as Karl Brugmann with an embarrassing dilemma; they caused him to hesitate to assign Goth. *ga-* to the IE morpheme to which in his opinion it phonologically belonged. He was quite certain that *ga-* was a reflex of the IE demonstrative pronominal stem **ghō*. But **ghō* is a highly deictic morpheme stressing the progression of an action from one point forward toward another and, as a verbal prefix, capable of expressing such ideas as those inherent in *von, zu, zu-, ver-,*[13] ideas which of course did not correspond to the static, reciprocal relationship expressed by *with, together*. These latter meanings which Brugmann naturally associated with *ga-* he acquired from the discussions of the morpheme that were current in his day: they were the only obstacle in the way of his certain conviction that *ga-* was a reflex of **ghō*: "Hinzuziehung des germ. Verbalpräfixes got. *ga-* kann höchstens des Sinnes wegen Bedenken erregen, weil wir historisch über die Bedeutung 'zusammen, mit' nicht hinauf kommen."[14]

---

[11] For a discussion of these logical "senses," see L. S. Stebbing, *A Modern Introduction to Logic* (London, 1953), pp. 111-15 and 166-74.

[12] *Deutsche Syntax*, p. 96.

[13] Karl Brugmann, *Die Demonstrativpronomina der indogermanischen Sprachen* (Leipzig, 1904), pp. 65-75, 116; Julius Pokorny, *Indogermanisches etymologisches Wörterbuch* (Bern and Munich, 1959), I, 451 f. Cf. also *IF*, xxxi, 97.

[14] Karl Brugmann und Berthold Delbrück, *Grundriss der vergleichenden Grammatik der indogermanischen Sprachen* (Strassburg, 1911), II, Part 2, pp. 847-49 (hereafter cited as Brugmann, *Grammatik*).

5. The fifth and final objection is a strictly linguistic one. It is based upon the fact that 'with,' 'together' are the conventional and normal translations of Lat. *cum* and that these meanings of *cum* are assigned to *ge-*, thereby willy-nilly commingling two different grammatical categories and their respective meanings. *Ge* - is a prefix, more specifically a preverb, and a morpheme that is simple; *cum* is presumably simple (although it may historically be a reflex of IE **ko* plus an instrumental morpheme, *m*), but it is a preposition. *With* is a preposition, while *together* is an adverb, and a compound one. Defining one of these grammatical categories in terms of several other different ones constitutes a kind of morphemic miscegenation conducive to results that one would expect to produce semantic chaos. *Ge-* may therefore be compared with Lat. *com-* because both are preverbs; it may not be compared with *cum* because the latter is a preposition, for, as Brøndal observes, the two grammatical categories present two different *systems*, a system of preverbs in a language and a system of prepositions. Co-existing as they do side by side they have at one and the same time different functions and different meanings. The meanings may remotely resemble one another, but they rarely or never precisely coincide. "Un systéme de prépositions ne se recouvrira jamais avec un systéme de préfixes dans un même état de langue."[15]

Preposition and Preverb

Because none of the extant literature on our morpheme has taken cognizance of the distinction between preposition and preverb, and because this distinction is essential to understanding both meaning and function of a preverb, it becomes necessary briefly to examine the nature of each.

Prepositions, like preverbs, presumably originally were adverbs, some of them from pronominal stems. In Indo-European these were originally autonomous, free morphemes, not necessarily confined to any fixed syntactic position. In the course of time the union of some adverbs with *nouns* was determined by a shift of syntactic elements, causing adverb and noun to achieve close proximity. Such adverbs in the main indicated spatial relationships; consequently they could be joined to the "oblique" or "adverbial" cases of nouns, i.e., all cases except the nominative and vocative. These cases were originally dependent directly on the verb, and the case-endings themselves adverbially modified that verb. When the adverb now fixed its position before the noun, became a "*pre*position," it merely made the verb-noun relationship clearer than that indicated by the case-ending. Finally, when syncretism of certain cases developed, the preposition then became imperative to indicate case relationships, as when in Latin the instrumental fell together with the ablative, and *cum* (originally with the instrumental) and *ab* (originally with the ablative) were the only indicators of the respective verb-noun

---

[15] Viggo Brøndal, *Théorie des prépositions* (Copenhagen, 1940).

relationship. The noun *plus* the preposition that "governs" it now becomes the modifier of the verb. It is because of such developments that in any given dialect at any given time the preposition is likely to be the indicator of a spatial relationship that is simple and concrete. But its function is *syntactic*.

The preverb, on the other hand, both in meaning and in function, is vastly different from a preposition. An adverb became a preverb when it and a *verb*, as immediate constituents of a syntactic unit, came to be regarded as a *lexical* unit. It is impossible to overemphasize this lexical nature of the preverb; preverb and verb consequently combine *semantically* ("Das Wesentliche ist dass Verbum und Adverbum begrifflich geeint sind"[16]). Historically they did not even have to be contiguous (Lat. *ob vos sacro* > *obsecro vos*; *sub vos placo* > *supplico vos*; *transque dato* > *traditoque*); generally even in Proto-Indo-European, they were contiguous, and the adverb preceded the verb. Depending upon the semantic nuances that might be desired, the preverb could be stressed or not stressed; in either case the preverb modified the verb, generally in terms of space; "... vermöge der ihr von Haus aus inne wohnenden Bedeutsamkeit dient die Präposition in Verbindung mit einem Verbum dazu, den Verbalbegriff *raümlich näher zu bestimmen*" (italics mine).[17] It is at this point, where the adverb becomes unstressed and a spatial modifier of its verb, a component of a lexical compound, that we may justly speak of it as a *preverb*. The union of the two morphemes then is not merely structural; essentially it is *lexical* and consequently semantic.

Moreover—and this is equally important—the preverb developed another distinctive semantic feature: whereas the preposition generally retained the single, concrete meaning of the original adverb, the preverb was more influenced by its environment, yielded some of its concreteness in being fused onto the verb, and consequently became more abstract. "Une membre inaccentué," says Brøndal, whose treatment of prepositions and prefixes is the most clarifying of any that I know, "donc internement léger aussi, offrira régulièrement un type d'emploi abstrait et un mode d'intuition formel. Aussi les prépositions employées comme preverbes, c.-à-d. comme premier terme (en général inaccentué) de composition verbal: *pour-chasser*. Nous avons manifestement ici le point de départ de l'évolution fréquent de préposition à préfixe où le préfixe est régulièrement beaucoup plus abstrait que la préposition originelle; cp. all. *er-*, *be-* ... et got. *us* 'hors de' ... *bi* 'pres de.'"[18] This kind of semantic mutation that takes place in the course of a change in position and stress one can easily illustrate even in modern English:

He *looked over* the wall ('He let his sight pass over the top of the wall').
(Concrete)

[16] Brugmann, *Grammatik*, II, pt. 2, p. 760.
[17] Brugmann, *Grammatik*, II, pt. 2, p. 771. Cf. A. Meillet, *Le slav commun* (Paris, 1934), p. 291.
[18] Brøndal, p. 79.

He *looked* the wall *over* ('He scrutinized the wall's area'). (Concrete)
He *overlooked* the wall ('He failed to take cognizance of the wall'). (Abstract)

He *threw* him *out* the window ('he forced him to the outside of the building'). (Concrete)
He *outthrew* him ('He threw better than the other'). (Abstract)

He *set* the sign *up* the road ('He placed the sign farther along the road'). (Concrete)
He *upset* the sign ('He caused the sign to fall'). (Abstract)

In sharp contrast then with a preposition which is single, concrete, and syntactic in function, the preverb is likely to be complex, abstract, and *lexical* in function. Brugmann was aware of such distinctions. That is why in his treatment of adverbial prepositions he discussed each under separate headings: under *A*. when he discussed it as a preverb, under *B*. when he discussed it as a preposition (*Grammatik*, II, pt. 2, 758-919).

In the light of the whole of the above discussion it ought by now to be apparent why one cannot in good conscience accept the prevailing Streitbergian hypothesis that the reflexes of PGmc. **ga-* became "empty" grammatical morphemes indicating aspect or that they could have meant the same as the Lat. preposition *cum*, meaning 'together,' 'with.' And if one cannot, can one anywhere in the literature pertaining to our morpheme find any respectable suggestions that might lead to some other explanation of its meaning and its function? One can, indeed. They are in the main observations and reflections, in some instances those of historical linguists of great stature, that have the one shortcoming that they lack the details of supporting evidence. It therefore becomes the burden of the remainder of this discussion to present these observations and *to try to supply enough evidence to establish their validity*. Needless to say, these observations are *not* reflected in the current grammars, handbooks, and dictionaries.

II

Over a century ago Jacob Grimm discussed *ge-* as a prefix extensively in his *Deutsche Grammatik*.[19] Very sensibly he avoids entangling it in anything approximating aspect or *Aktionsart* and supports his observations by many examples from most of the Germanic dialects. His observations on the prefix as a preverb one may reduce to three principal ones that are simple and clear:
1. *ge-* corresponds to Lat. *com-*, *con-*, *co-*, and like these it modifies the simplex with which it is joined, modifies it markedly if it is a strong verb (p. 819).
2. Frequently it adds to the action expressed by such a compound the idea of duration and continuity (p. 821)—an observation for which there is abundant

---

[19] Jacob Grimm, *Deutsche Grammatik*, 2nd ed., as revised by Scherer (Berlin, 1878), II.

evidence in the OE Matthew and *Orosius*, but an observation that Streitberg rejected because it would have denied his own hypothesis its very foundation. 3. The meaning of *ge-* is related to that of HG *er-* and *be-* (p. 828). Further than that he does not commit himself with regard to meaning in his discussion of the morpheme as a preverb, and never does he suggest that it meant 'with,' 'together.'

Grimm's discussion of the prefix as a preverb is thus in the main descriptive, and we get little or no commitment from him that would reveal what he believed to be its lexical meaning. However, when we go back to his discussion of the prefix in the nominal declension, there we discover it, briefly and unostentatiously recorded, lost, almost, in a sea of surrounding typography, and dormant apparently for over a century. For nowhere in the literature on our morpheme, in not one of the some thirty-five dissertations, monographs, and articles, nor in any of the grammars and handbooks, do we find it mentioned. Yet it is there, on page 738 of Scherer's edition, brief, terse, and heavy with implications for our purpose, even though negatively stated: "Gegensatz ist *ab-*."

Now if in Grimm's particular and native idiom the lexical "Gegensatz" of the morpheme is 'off-' then the meaning of *ge-* would have to be 'on-' or 'to-,' or both: *abbringen—anbringen*; *ablegen—anlegen*; *ableiten—zuleiten*; *abreden—zureden*.

To illustrate his conviction that "Gegensatz ist *ab-*" Grimm continues: "vgl. ab-hâr (depilis) mit ge-hâr (gleichsam com-pilis). In den übrigen fällen schwächerer bedeutung wechselt ge- mit be, z. b. gi-zengi, bi-tengi; ge-sceid, be-scheid; ge-derbe, bederbe; ags. ge-leáfa, engl. be-lief; es ist wie be- und ver- zuweilen inhaltsleer geworden, *ursprünglich nicht gewesen*" (p. 738, italics mine). Adjectives when prefixed with *ge-* indicate that the thing or the characteristic expressed by the stem is applied to the noun that the compound modifies: "ge-hâr (crinitus)"; "ge-hende (propinquus) *zur* hand, behend" (pp. 734–36). Furthermore, the *ge-* prefixed to adverbs he also refrains from translating with *mit* or *zusammen*, generally translating it with a morpheme having an asymmetrical—transitive sense, expressing continuing sequence: "gi-tago (quotidie)" 'day *by* day'; "gi-zîto (mature)" '*at* the proper time'; or else what Pott called "eine durchgehende Erstreckung über eine distribuierte Allheit": "ge-slago (consequenter) schlag *auf* schlag, ge-orto (mit dem ort, dem apex, der spitze *an* einander stossend) gesîto (seite *an* seite)."[20] Grimm recognizes the tradition that says that *ge-* may be similar in meaning to "lat. cum, con-" but he does not pursue it and recognizes the phonological difficulties that stand in the way of such a correlation.

August Pott also believed that the meaning of *ge-* was something quite

---

[20] Jacob Grimm, *Deutsche Grammatik* (Göttingen, 1831), III, 158; A. F. Pott, *Etymologische Forschungen auf dem Gebiete der indogermanischen Sprachen* (Lemgo and Detmold, 1859), p. 852.

different from 'together' or 'with' and agrees in the main with Grimm. "Ahd. galauba ... und galaubo ... und galaubi ... nebst Ahd. und Goth. galaubjan (credere) helfen in dem *ga-* auch wohl die *Hingabe* an das geglaubte hervorheben" (p. 856). *Giuellet* to him means 'obuenerit,' and *gafelli* means "*zu*fall." "Galîdan ... ist peregrinari, cedere, allein auch, was sich mit dem *ga-* als zusammen wenig zu reimen scheint, als *Hinweg*: exire, excedere ... u.s.w." (p. 857, italics mine).

Moreover, among the writers in the nineteenth century there are some others whom our literature has ignored and whose observations may justly be regarded as pertinent to the clarification of our morpheme; these are the scholars of Old Norse. Old Norse has been neglected in attempts to evaluate the significance of the morpheme on the assumption that *ge-* does not appear in the literature of that dialect. However, it was in the language before the written literature appeared, and even in the literature itself it survived in a syncopated form as *g-* in many words, such as *glikr*. In its full form as a preverb it was lost. The prevailing theory explaining this loss, supported by Kuhn, Heusler, and Dal, is that it had to compete with eleven other older preverbs in Old Norse, and lost; finally only one of all these preverbs survived, namely *of-*. But according to Kuhn all of these preverbs were practically equal in meaning and could perform almost identical functions. "Schon zu der Zeit aber, als die schwachen Vorsilben noch bestanden [c. 850 A.D.] konnten sie unterschiedslos ersetzt werden durch die Partikel *of-* (got. *uf*)."[21] "Darum," says Kuhn, "stehen *of likr* und *glikr* neben einander."[22] Scholars of Old Norse agree that *of-* had meaning: Heusler reads "*über ... hin, an,*" Brugmann "*an, in, über*" (i.e., not 'above' but 'over to'); DeVries reads "*auf, über, zu.*"[23]

If we now pass down into the busy intellectual activity of the Renaissance we encounter another writer of some linguistic competence who took occasion to comment on our preverb. Him, too, our recent scholarship has overlooked. True, one cannot approach him with quite so much assurance as one could the disciplined and thoroughly trained linguists of the nineteenth century whom I discussed above; yet neither can one superciliously ignore him, for he had some firsthand knowledge that they probably did not possess and he was four hundred years nearer to the older dialects than we are. He was Johannes van Gorp, better known at Goropius and Becanus, and he was a physician in the Low Countries who gave up a successful and lucrative practice in order to devote all his time to the study of languages. His works were published in Antwerp in 1580. His etymologies are subjective and sometimes contrived; yet he knew Latin, Greek, and Hebrew well, was the first to publish the Gothic Lord's Prayer as he found it in the Codex Argenteus, and, what is of

---

[21] Andreas Heusler, *Altisländisches Elementarbuch* (Heidelberg, 1962), p. 41.
[22] Hans Kuhn, *Das Füllwort of- um im Altwestnordischen* (Göttingen, 1924), p. 99.
[23] Jan DeVries, *Altnordisches Etymologisches Wörterbuch* (Leiden, 1961), p. 416.

greater importance to us, was intensely interested in the Germanic dialect of his own province—Brabant.

Becanus finds occasion to comment upon *ge-* frequently throughout his *Hermathena*. The following are typical and, if accurate, as I believe they are, illuminating examples: "Hinc sit vt *Ge* aliquando pro *Ad* Latinorum usurpemus: vt si quis dicat Ge Louen / id est, ad Louanium vel Louanium versus."[24] His examples for the prefix in the nominal declension are convincing: "*ge-* / ad significat ut sit ge-ew / ad aeternitatem; geheb / id est, ad habendum dicitur; gehef / id est, ad eleuandum" (p. 116), and the examples that he gives us of the prefix as a preverb suggest the "hinweg" of Pott, "Gerect / id est extensum" (p. 228), or they illustrate his observation that *ge-* prefixed to a verb indicates that the action expressed by that verb is "more carried out" (the earliest statement that I have found that asserts that *ge-* "perfectivates"): "Additur eadem vocula in compositione, ad perfectiorem quoque significationem, extra praeteritum perfectum. Sic *doen*, est agere: *gedoen*, agendo sibi quidquam perficerè" (p. 138). On p. 215 he repeats his original observation: "*Ge* idem est quod Latinus dicit *versus* sive *ad*" (italics mine).

To the above list we must add the name of Eduard Sievers. Although Sievers apparently never discussed the preverb in print and never suggested any specific meaning for the morpheme, he belongs here because, according to one of his students, he questioned the utility of trying to explain a morpheme in terms of the *Aktionsarten*.[25] Sievers believed that the Anglo-Saxon writers were not interested essentially in expressing the *Aktionsarten* but they used the simplex verb for the purpose of "Konstatierung" (simply stating an unqualified action) and the prefixed compound for purposes of "Betrachtung und Schilderung" (which can only mean modifying an action in such a way, generally in terms of space, in order to make it more descriptive.)

From the discussion immediately above it is quite apparent that this group of writers differs considerably in its interpretation of *ge-* from Streitberg. Above all, these question or ignore it as a marker of a gramatical category and insist that it had lexical meaning—Grimm stating that it meant 'an, zu' and that it was related to *be-* and *er-*; Pott suggesting 'hin, hinweg'; the scholars of Old Norse observing that its surrogate *of-* meant 'über-hin,' 'an,' 'auf,' and 'zu;' and Goropius informing us that in his own dialect it was at times equivalent to Lat. *ad*. The semantic variations here are not of great moment; as I shall show later, they are reconcilable. What is of greater moment— and what we have to come to terms with—is Grimm's observation that "*ge-* entspricht dem lat. *com-*"; and we have to come to terms with it because there are still too many utterances currently abroad that insist or imply that *com-* is identical in meaning with *cum*, a position that is no longer tenable.

---

[24] Joannes Goropius, *Hermathena* (Antwerp, 1580), p. 137.
[25] Alfred Wuth, *Aktionsarten der Verba bei Cynewulf* (diss., Weida i. Thür., 1915), pp. 12–14.

Com- and *cum*

Com- and *cum*, semantically, are not the same. One of the reasons why they are not I stated in Paragraph 5 under the objections to Streitberg's hypothesis, namely, that the former is a preverb and the latter a preposition, consequently different in nature and different in function. In mild censure of some grammarians of an older school, Brøndal expresses this a bit differently:

> La querelle rappelée plus haut sur les prépositions séperables et inséperables est due au fait qu'il y a souvent contact ou parenté entre préposition et préfixe:
> Prépositions et préfixes se présent souvent comme des doublets, c.-à-d. comme deux formes de même origine, dont l'une est préposition indépendante (lat. *cum*. fr. *pour*), l'autre préfixe non autonome (lat. *com*-, fr. *pro*-).
> Ces faits ont, jusque de nos jours, mené les grammairiens à de graves confusions:
> 1. D'authentiques préfixes ont été traités comme des prépositions inséperables....
> 2. D'authentiques prépositions sont par contre présentees comme des préfixes....
> 3. Enfin on considère comme synonymes les doublets du type indiqué plus haut; ainsi pour lat. *com*- et *cum* (Bréal), dont on ne voyait pas l'appartenance respective à des systèmes differents: *com*- correlatif d'éléments morphologiques abstraits comme *dis*- et *re*-; *cum* par contre corrélatif de mots essentiellement plus lourds comme *apud, coram,* et *penes*.[26]

Hugo Weber, as early as 1890, detected these same distinctions: "Sed id quidem hic ponere liceat praefixam illam particulam com (con-) nec per originem nec per notionis proprietatum omnino quidquam commune habere cum praepositionis 'cum' quae vulgo eadem esse vox atque illa creditur."[27]

Indo-Europeanists themselves are not agreed on the origins of *com*- and *cum*, but the majority of them regard both as reflexes of IE **ko* or **kom*. But even **kom* did not exclusively mean 'together,' 'with,' even when used as a preposition; it could mean 'apud, iuxta,' and in Umbrian, where it appears as *-ku* and denotes rest, it is translated by Lat. *ad*.[28] Originally it appears to have expressed direction: 'an etwas entlang.' According to Brugmann the form **ko*, which appears primarily in verbal compounds, is the morpheme that generated Old Irish *co*, meaning 'to.' And even when Brugmann discusses **kom*, he makes an important and probably often ignored distinction when, in terms of 'zusammen,' he explains its meaning as a preverb or as a preposition; as a preposition it means "das lokale Zusammen*sein*," but as a preverb it means "ein Zusammen*kommen*" (p. 853, italics mine). And therein lies a world of difference.

Among Latinists of the twentieth century it is Erik Ahlmann who substantiates the views expressed above by Brøndal and Weber. He finds that there must necessarily be *two* readings of the preverb *com*-, one when it is

---

[26] Brøndal, p. 12.
[27] Hugo Weber, *Questiones Catullianae* (Gotha, 1890), p. 31.
[28] Brugmann, *Grammatik*, II, pt. 2, pp. 851–55.

prefixed to verbs indicating a situation of rest, another when it is prefixed to verbs of motion. When the verb indicates a situation of rest, then *com-* must be translated not with *together* but with Lat. *una* or *simul* 'at the same place, at the same time.' But when the verb indicates motion, the *com-* must be translated by a morpheme whose meaning approximates 'to.' For *com-* now has "die schon angedeutete, mit der Bedeutung von *ad-* verwandte, mit terminus quo verbundene Funktion."[29] And in such a situation, depending on the *meaning* of the verb, the *kind* of motion that it expresses, it can also have the function of indicating a "terminus unde," in which case verbs like *concedo* and *confugo* will mean 'go away', 'flee from, away,' without necessarily stating any other goal.

The operation of this terminative and directional function of *com-* Ahlmann illustrates with certain denominative verbs that indicate that an object has affixed to it that which is expressed by the original noun: "*collaudo* (= 'laude afficio' vgl. d. *berühmen*); *consaluto* (d. *begrüssen*); *condemno* (= 'damno afficio' d. *bestrafen*); *collumino* (d. *beleuchten*)" (p. 95). One might add here that in the OHG glosses the preverb that, besides *gi*, most frequently translates Lat. *com-* is *pi-* (meaning not 'around,' like the preposition, but 'on' and 'on to'). The same function, Ahlmann continues, is apparent in verbs that are not denominative: "*coaedificio-bebauen*; *compingo-bemalen*; *conspergo-besprengen*." "*Congredi aliquem*" in Plautus is "*adgredi aliquem* in classical Latin; *collator* means '*be*bellen,' and *concredo* means '*an*vertrauen' (pp. 96-100). One could greatly increase the number of such examples.

These functions of *com-* Ahlmann calls terminative (though in many cases they are merely deictic), and he is somewhat at a loss to account for this function. It cannot, he says, have grown out of the meaning 'zusammen, una,' first because the purely rest-meaning 'together' appears only rarely in early Latin literature, second because a rest-meaning does not normally develop into a terminative meaning. The terminate meaning he regards as the older of the two, and he believes that the morpheme in this earlier period had a meaning similar to Lat. *ad-*: "Eine einfachere Erklärung erhalten diese Verba, when wir annehmen, dass die Bed. von *com-* früher umfassender gewesen ist, etwa *ad-*" (pp. 113-16).

R. Köstler, writing in 1951, is of the same opinion, and bases this opinion upon a study of early Roman legal terminology. He holds that, although the preverb *com-* in classical Latin is often translated with *zusammen* or *mit*, these meanings did not apply in the earlier period of the patricians and plebes; in this period *com-* meant 'to' or 'thereto' ("*zu* oder *dazu*"). *Coemere* meant '*an*kaufen'; *coemptia* meant '*zu*kauf.' New members of the senate chosen from the plebes rather than from the established patricians were called *conscripti*,

---

[29] Erik Ahlman, *Über das lateinische Präfix* com- *in Verbalzusammensetzungen* (Helsingfors, 1916), p. 59.

"*zu*geschriebene." "Cognatus ist nicht der Mitgeborene sondern der der bisherigen Familie Zugeborene und durch die Zugeburt Blutsverwandt." The meaning of 'to' for *com-* he finds still surviving in classical Latin in such words as *consentire, cooptare,* and *consequi,* and he believes that in the earlier period *com-* was generally preferred to *ad-*; *contaminare* becomes late Latin *attaminare.*[30]

The above discussion of *com-* does not, of course, presume to suggest that OE *ge-* is cognate with *com*; such suggestion has long been rejected on phonological grounds—despite Bugge's efforts to postulate a Germanic /g/ that would correspond to an initial Latin /k/ by means of subtle applications of Verner's Law.[31] (A normal Germanic phonological equivalent of *com-* would have to be something like NLG *hen,* NHG *hin.*) Rather, the above discussion indicates that the *meaning* of *com-* is consistent with the rest of the meanings proposed by Grimm and the other writers treated in this section and that, above all, there is no semantic inconsistency in the fact that the Old English translations of Matthew reveal that *ge-* compounds just as frequently translate Latin compounds in *ad-* as they do those in *com-*, as previously stated:

	C.	R.	L.
ad-	46.1%	42.3%	61.5%
com-	37.1%	42.8%	62.8%

III

Because a preverb normally "offrira régulièrement un type d'emploi abstrait et un mode d'intuition formel," i.e., does not express an "intuition réelle" (like a concrete location) but a *relation* that is abstract, formal, and logical, many preverbs can express similar relations and, if they are genuine prefixes, can even be substituted one for another. This has always held generally true for the Germanic dialects, as witness NE *believe* and NHG *g(e)lauben,* or NHG and Modern Dutch pairs like *Erzählung-vertaling, erlösen-verlossen, gehört-behoort,* etc. The practice was apparently widespread in the earlier Germanic dialects and there had inestimable relevance to the clarification of our morpheme. P. Pietsch called attention to this practice nearly a century ago when he observed that in Old High German one writer might prefix certain verbs with *ge-* while some other contemporaneous writer might not; the latter might prefix those same verbs with some other preverb. However, in both instances, the respective compounds would "mean" the same. According to Pietsch the choice of the different preverbs was due to dialectal and ideolectal habits

---

[30] R. Köstler, "Com = (da) zu," *Glotta,* XXXI (1951), 121–27.
[31] S. Bugge, "Etymologische studien über germanische lautverschiebung," *PBB,* XII (1889), 413–21.

or conventions.[32] Mossé repeats the observation: "La seconde conclusion plus importante à nos yeux et de plus grande conséquence comme on va le voir, c'est que beaucoup de ces préverbes étaient interchangeables."[33] "Im Schwäbischen," writes a lexicographer discussing the preverb *be-*, "wird es' mitunter ... durch andere präfixe wie *ge-* und *ver-* vertreten."[34] "An stelle von *ga-*," says Hirt, "tritt im Deutschen später *er* (g. *us*)."[35] If we now turn to the three OE dialect translations of the Vulgate Gospel According to Saint Matthew, we shall see that the above practice is very much in evidence there also.

The following sets of inter-dialectal substitutions or correspondences are typical of the whole corpus. One might note in passing that in sets 1 and 3 the functions of the preverbs are quite different from those of the prepositions and situatives that follow the compound; they lack the concreteness or precision of the latter.

1. 6:27, quis ... potest *adicere ad* staturam suam
   C.   *ge*-eacnige to
   R.   *æt*-ece to
   L.   æt ł *to*-ece to

2. 26:45, ecce *appropinquauit* hora
   C.   *ge*nealæcð
   R.   *to*-neoliceþ
   L.   *ge*neoleces

3. 27:60, et *aduoluit* saxum ... *ad* ostium
   C.   *to*-awylte   to
   R.   *to*-wælde   to
   L.   *ge*wælte   to

4. 23:5, *dilatant* enim philacteria sua
   C.   *to*-brædaþ
   R.   brædaþ
   L.   *ge*brædas

5. 4:8, et *ostendit* ei omnia regna mundi
   C.   *æt*-eowde
   R.   *æt*-eawde
   L.   *ge*-eaude

[32] P. Pietsch, "Einige Bermerkungen ueber *ge-* bei Verben," *PBB*, XII (1889), 516–29.
[33] Mossé, *Histoire*, II, 23.
[34] *Trübner's deutsches Wörterbuch* (Berlin, 1939), I, 247, col. 2.
[35] Hermann Hirt, *Handbuch des Urgermanischen* (Heidelberg, 1934), II, 134.

It is time to pause for a moment in order to recapitulate and synthesize the observations made in Section II above and in Section III up to this point. If we now restate the opinions and inferences of Grimm, Pott, Goropius, Kuhn, Heusler, Brugmann, Ahlmann, and Koestler, namely, that *ge-* meant 'an, zu, hin, hinweg, über-hin, auf, be-, er-, ad,' add to these the fact that our data show that *ge-* corresponded primarily to such Latin preverbs as *ad-*, *com-*, *in-*, and *ex-*, add to all of these the fact that *ge-* compounds in one Old English dialect corresponded to compounds in *a-*, *be-*, ("*be-* a le sense de 'sur'"),[36] *for-*, *forþ-*, *on-*, and *to-* in the other Old English dialects, then we see that the data corroborate the observations and opinions of the grammarians, and both provide us with a fairly substantial background against which to view and reevaluate the function and meaning of OE *ge-*.

Expressing relations is admittedly the only concern of preverbs; and inasmuch as relations are abstractions of logic, only the terminology of logic can explain them. According to such terminology all relations have a *sense*, a direction in which a relation goes. If between two terms the relation goes both ways, is reversible, or reciprocal, that is, if *y* is related to *x* in the same way that *x* is related to *y*, then the sense is *symmetrical* (⇌); if not, the sense is *asymmetrical*. If on the other hand the direction goes one way and can be *prolonged*, it is *transitive* (and imperfective) (→); if not, it is *intransitive* (and perfective) (⊢→). These senses may be illustrated by the following prepositions: the relation expressed by *together* or *with* is symmetrical—transitive; by *on*, as in "He staggered on," or *toward* is asymmetrical—transitive (and imperfective); by *to*, indicating arrival at a goal, as in "He came to my house," is asymmetrical—intransitive (and perfective).[37]

Serious reflection upon the preverbs included in the correlations that I have just discussed two paragraphs above will reveal that the "sense" of all of them is asymmetrical; they express a relation that moves forward and outward *only*. In some instances they are transitive, in others intransitive. To correspond with all of these, *ge-* would have had to be asymmetrical also, and capable of expressing both transitivity *and* intransitivity. Like the IE **gho-* of which it is a reflex, it, too, is deictic; it points to a way through *space*. To state the implications of all this in the form of a proposition will give us its "meaning."

To state the meaning of a morpheme it is not necessary to become involved in what Hjelmslev called "transcendental linguistics," or in the psycholinguistic section of semasiology, or in the contradictions of the behaviorist's notion that meaning is a "response." It is sufficient to operate on a generally accepted and simple principle of semantics, namely that the "meaning" of a morpheme is whatever entity or concept the *consensus gentium* of any given speech community at any given time has correlated with a given acoustic sign.

---

[36] Mossé, *Histoire*, II, 6.
[37] Stebbing, pp. 38, 111–15. Cf. Brøndal, p. 34.

"Meaning" of the Morpheme 37

Consequently, in the light of the correspondences established above OE preverbal *ge-* would have to "mean" that '*the action expressed by any verb to which it is prefixed is directed toward some thing or in a direction forward and outward.*' This is what the correlations tell us. And this is the meaning that Lorz adumbrated without documentation when he said: "Seine Grundbedeutung ist 'vorwärts'."[38] Moreover, this is merely a more precise statement of what Holgar Pederson found for another reflex of IE **gho-*, namely Armenian *z*: "Ebenso bezeichnet *z* den weg einer bewegung."[39]

This meaning of *ge-* as I have stated it above I would call its *abstract meaning*, and is its semantic nucleus. It is what Ullmann would call the "core" of the meaning, what Brøndal would call the "signification centrale," what v. Wartburg regards as the "umgrenzter Kern," and what Schmidt would regard as the "locus" of all "actualized meanings." In and among the bundle of potential and variable contextual meanings of a morpheme this semantic nucleus is a stable element, never expressed, that is imbedded in the linguistic system, in the "langue"; and the so-called contextual meanings can never be anything more than particular applications of this semantic "core" that develop in the utterances of the "parole." Add such a semantic nucleus to the contextual meaning of the morpheme and *the nucleus, the abstract meaning, will invariably be redundant*. One NE morpheme alone will not suffice to express this abstract meaning in all contexts. As we shall see below, the NE morphemes necessary to translate this abstract meaning of *ge-* will be such morphemes as *at, on, to, toward,* and *out, forth, away.*

The question that now arises is whether or not this semantic nucleus is reflected in and substantiated by the *contextual meanings* and correspondences of our texts, and whether or not it appears so consistently as a correlative of *ge-* that one can regard it as a semantically stable element of Old English considered as a "langue." For such purposes an examination of only 9,000 instances of verbs limited to only three OE dialects seemed not sufficiently convincing; to establish the meaning clearly, I considered it necessary to extend the collations to versions of Matthew, available only to a limited extent, in the other Germanic dialects. This enlarged the number of verbs examined, both simplex and compound, to 45,000, and therefore not only increased the number of contexts of utterances but also more firmly established the "contexts of intent"—contexts that must be absolutely clear in order to determine what a morpheme in such a context is *supposed* to express, assuming always that the translators were dedicated to their task and cognizant of a well-established convention of Biblical idiom.

[38] Ant. Lorz, *Aktionsarten des Verbums im Beowulf* (Würzburg, 1908), p. 16.
[39] Holger Pedersen, "Armenisch und die Nachbarsprachen," *Zeitschrift für Vergleichende Sprachforschung*, xxxix (Neue Folge xix) (1906), 435. For Armenian *z* as a reflex of **gho*, see Brugmann, *Grundriss*, ii, pt. 2, p. 347, and A. Meillet, "Étymologies slaves," *Mémoires de la Société de Linguistique de Paris*, ix (1896), 53.

Consequently, in the chart below, I continue with the Old English sets of correspondences that I introduced briefly above. These appear in the left-hand column under the Latin words that they translate and that are arranged alphabetically according to their *stems*, not their prefixes. To the right of each of these sets are the extended collations from the other Germanic dialects, chosen from the versions of Matthew that were as close in time to the Old English ones as possible and from those that represented as much geographical latitude as the available documents permitted, the Middle Low German ones having to act as substitutes for an Old Saxon version that does not exist. Gothic is added merely to reveal that the "idioms" expressed by the other dialects were already apparent in this dialect also. The texts that yielded these latter collations are: 1. the Old High German *Monsee Fragments* (M.),[40] 2. the Old High German *Tatian* (T.),[41] 3. the Middle Low German *Bibel* printed in Cologne in c. 1478 (K.),[42] 4. the Middle Low German Quatuor Evangeliorum versio Saxonica, MS Thott 8,8,° of the Kongelige Bibliotek, Copenhagen (Th.),[43] 5. Oddur Gotskalkson's Icelandic *Hið Nya Testament* (I.)[44] and 6. Streitberg's *Die gotische Bibel* (G.).[45] The passages from the Wycliffite *Bibel* (Wyc.) suggest that some OE idioms survived into late Middle English.[46] The contextual material may be divided into two general classes, both mandatory as evidence for the meaning.

I. Ge- *corresponds to preverbs, prepositions, or adverbs that can be translated by morphemes meaning 'at, on, to, toward,' or 'be-.'*

The evidence here has to be extensive in order to demonstrate the semantic stability of the prefix regardless of its morphemic and contextual environment. My own interpretations of the *original* meaning of some of the OE compounds are conjectures drawn from analogy with the collations.

    1. 5:41, angariaberit
        C. swa hwa þe *genyt*   I. þreyngdu *til*
        L.   *genedes*   G. *ana*nauþjai
    A denominative verb, therefore 'so anyone put need *on to* you'

[40] George Allison Hench, *The Monsee Fragments* (Strassburg, 1890).

[41] *Tatian*, ed. Eduard Sievers (Paderborn, 1960). This is a reprint of the second edition of 1892.

[42] No title page. There were two LG Bibles printed in Cologne about 1478, K^u and K^e. According to internal evidence K^u is slightly earlier than K^e. I have followed K^u.

[43] As far as I have been able to determine this MS has never been published or edited *in toto*. A description of it, a few extracts, and a glossary were published as an inaugural dissertation: Max Weber, *Die mitteldeutschen Evangelien in der Handschrift der Grossen Kgl. Bibliothek zu Kopenhagen* (Greifswald, 1908).

[44] Oddur Gottskalkson, *Hið Nya Testament, 1540*, in *Monumenta Typographica Islandica*, ed. Sigurður Nordal (Copenhagen, 1933), 1.

[45] *Die gotische Bibel*, ed. Wilhelm Streitberg (Heidelberg, 1960).

[46] John Wycliffe and His Followers, *The Holy Bible*, ed. J. Forshall and F. Madden (Oxford, 1850).

"Meaning" of the Morpheme

2. 7:24, audit
   C. e ðas mine word *gehyrð*   T. gihorit
                                       ("anhört")
   R.   *ge-héreð*   K. darhort
   L.   *geheres*   Th. dar horet
                                    I. atheyragt
                                       (27.14)

   Our forefathers regarded many verbs of sense-perception such as *to see* and *to hear* as verbs of motion. Here an *intransitive* verb + ge + acc. object; therefore 'Who hears *on to* my words.' Cf. note s.v. *vident*, no. 120 below.

3. 10:38, accipit
   C. se þe ne nimþ hys cwylminge
   R.   *genimaþ*   T. inphahit
   L.   onfoeð   Th. up nemet
                                    I. tekr a sig

   'He who does not take *to* (himself) his suffering'

4. 8:17, accepit
   C. He onfeng ure untrumnessa   T. inphing
   R.   onfeng   K. benamen
   L.   *genom*   I. uppa sig tekit
                                    G. usnam
                                       ("annehmen")

   'Took on'

5. 27:48, acceptam
   C. án heora ... *genam* ane spongeam   T. intfangana
   R.   *genom*   I. til tok
   L.   *genóm*

6. 6:2, receperunt
   C. hi *onfengon* hyra mede   T. intphiengun
   R.   *onfengon*   ("zu sich
   L.   *gefengon*   nehmen")
                                    K. entfangen
                                    Th. entfingen
                                    I. ut tekit
                                    G. andnemun
                                       ("an-
                                       aufnehmen")

7. 17:7, accesit
    C. He *genealæhte* þa   T. zuogieng
    R.   eode   Th. gink to
    L.   *genealecde*   I. gieck til
                                        I. gieck at (25:22)

8. 9:20, ─────
    C. án wif *genealæhte* wið-æftan   K. ginck by eme
    R.   *geneolicde*   Th. gink em to
    L.   *geneolecde*   I. gieck til vid
                                         G. duatgaggandei duatiddja (7:5)

    Transitive sense; Th. "gink em to" does *not* mean 'went *to* him' but 'went *toward* him,' like NHG "ging auf ihn *zu*."
    Wyc. "*cam to* byhynde"

9. 24:1, ─────
    C. him tó-*genealæhton* hys leorning-cnihtes   T. zuogiengen
    R.   eoden *to*   M. gingen to
    L.   to-*geneolecdon*   I. geingu til

    In such decomposita as those above where *ge-* appears to be *in tmesi*, the *to* is a true *preposition*, not a preverb, and indicates that the goal of the approach has been reached. These express a relation that is asymmetrical and *intransitive* and, consequently, true perfectivity, the reaching of the goal, which the *ge-* per se apparently does not express.
    Wyc. "camen nig"

10. 7:19, accedens
    C. Ða *genealæhte* him an bocere   T. gieng zuo
    R.   cumende   K. genck tho
    L.   *genealacde*   Th. gink to
                                      I. giek at
                                      G. duatgaggands
    Wyc. "And oo scribe, *commynge to* [no *him*], saide to hym"

11. 28:2, ─────
    C. drihtenes engel ... *genealæhte*   T. zuogangenti
    R.   *to*gangende   Th. gink to
    L.   *geneolecde*   I. giek til

    Here the *to* in R. *is* a preverb. Out of 42 instances of some form of *accedere* R. translates with *geneolican* only twice. Otherwise he uses *togan* or a simplex.
    Wyc. "and *comynge to* turnide away the stoon"

"Meaning" of the Morpheme

12. 7:24, audit
    C. ælc þæra þe ðas mine word *gehyrð*   T. gihórit ("anhört")
    R.   *ge-héreð*   K. dar hort
    L.   *geheres*   Th. dar horet
    Intransitive verb + *ge-* + acc. object. Therefore, like T., 'hear *on to* my words'

13. 23:13, clauditis
    C. ge *beluca*ð heofona rice   T. bisliozet
    R.   *ge*lucaþ   K. besluten
        I. aptr lokit

    "Commutation principle"

14. 8:20, reclinet
    C. mannes sunu næfð hwær
        he hys heafod   *ahylde*   T. inthelde
    R.   *ahélde*   K. an rowe
    L.   *gehlutes* ł *gebeges*   Th. to noghe
        I. at hneigi
        G. anahnaiwjai

    Luther: "hin lege"

15. 8:28, occurrerunt
    C. þa *urnon* him *togenes* twegen   T. ingegin liofun
    R.   *urnon*   *ongean*   K. begenden
    L.   *ge-uurnon* him [no *ongean*]   I. lupu i moti
        G. gamotidedun ("begegnen")

    Despite the *ge-*, *ge-uurnon* remains a durative, intransitive verb because it "governs" a dative, not an accusative: 'ran forth [to him].'

16. Cf. Mark 9:15, accurentes
    C. 7 hine gretende him *to urnon*
    L. 7 *geuurnon* groeton hine   T. zuolaufante
        G. durinnandans

    Here, in L., there is no dative goal, therefore merely 'they ran forth.' Wyc. "and thei *rennynge to*, greeten him"

17. 27:64, custodiri
    C. hat nu haldan þa byrgene   T. bihaltanne
    R.   *gehaldan*   K. bewaren
    L.   *gehalda*   Th. bewaren
        I. forware

    Continuous action: 'guard,' i.e., 'hold forth,' i.e., 'continue to hold'

18. 24:10, tradent
    C. manega ... belæwað betwyx him   K. vorraden
    R.   sellað   Th. vorraden
    L.   geseallas   I. ofer selia

19. 18:34, tradidit
    C. 7 *sealde* hine þam witnerum
    R.   salde
    L.   gesalde   I. ofer selldi

20. 26:2, traditur
    C. wite geþ ... mannes bearn *byð geseald*   T. giselit
    R.   *bið sald*   K. averghelevert
    L.   *gesald bið*   I. overseliagt
                                                  G. at gibida ("hin-
                                                     übergegeben")

Despite the past-participial construction, not just 'will be given' but 'will be given *over*'!

The preceding three sets clearly reveal a few pertinent facts about *ge*-: 1. it has nothing to do with tenses; 2. as has long been known, and as the last set again reminds us, it was not mandatory as a constituent of the past participle; in other words it had *no* grammatical function; 3. the distinction between *sellan* and *gesellan* is lexical—they are two different words—and the function of the prefix is to add concretion. *Sellan* expresses the simple unconnected act of 'giving'; *gesellan* means 'to give over,' 'to hand over,' and is the more descriptive. This is precisely the distinction that Eduard Sievers made when he said that in his opinion the Anglo-Saxon writer was not interested in expressing the *Aktionsarten* but that to him the simplex was "constatierend" whereas the compound was "schilderned." *Consequently the prefix was never mandatory*; it could be used in general at the discretion of the writer, depending upon whether he wanted to make a general statement or a specific descriptive one. (At a relatively late date some compounds became conventionalized.) This freedom of choice is especially well illustrated in the following two sets:

21. 21:2, adducite
    C. untigeað hig 7 lædeð to mé   T. *gileitet* mir
    R.   ledað   I. leidit til min
    L.   *to-lædes*

    Cf. Mark 11:2,
    C. untigeað hine 7 to me *gelædað*   G. attiuhat
                                                   ("herbeiführen")

    'Lead him forth'

"Meaning" of the Morpheme

22. 15:37, tulerunt
    C. þ to lafe wæs ... hig namon
    R.   *genomon*   K. houen vp
    L.   *genomon*   I. toku vpp,

23. Cf. Mark 12:16, at illi attulerunt [denarium]
    R. soð hiæ *gibrohton* [pening]   G. at berun
    L. soþ hia *to-brohton*
    "Commutation principle"

24. 14:35, optulerunt
    C. hi *brohton to* him ealle úntrume   Th. brohten vor
    L.   *gebrohton* him   I. foerdu til

25. 8:16, ――――
    C. hig brohton him manege defol-seoce
    L.   *gebrohton*   K. brohton vor
           I. foerdu til
           G. atberun
             ("darbringen")

26. 19:5, adhaerebit
    C. se mann ... hyne to hys wife *geþ eot*   T. zuoclebet
    R.   *aet*-clifað wife   K. anhangen
    L.   *genehuas* wife   Th. tohangen

27. 6:27, adicere
    C. þ he *ge-eacnige* ane elne to his anlicness   T. zuogiouban
    R.   *æt-ece*   K. tho tho geueen
           G. anaaukan
             ("hinzufügen")

Wyc. "*putte to* to his stature oo cubite?"

28. 26:50, iniecerunt
    C. hig ... þone haeland *genamon*   T. legitun ire hant *in*
              then heilant *ana*
    R.   *genamun*
    L.   *geworpun ... on*

29. 21:21, ire (hierosolymam)
    C. þ he wolde *faran to* hierusalem   K. gan to
    R.   *færan to*   Th. gaen to
    L.   *gegæ* hierusalem   I. ganga til
    Not 'to get Jerusalem by going' but simply 'to go to Jerusalem,' or, 'to go *on to* Jerusalem.' Intrans. verb + *ge-* + acc. object

30. 6:6, ora
   C. bide þinne fæder on dihlum
   R. bidde
   L. *gebidd*   K. bede tho
                                              Th. an bede

   Luther: "bete zu"

31. 2:8, adorem
   C. Þic ... me to him *gebidde*   K. anbede
   R.   *gebidde*   Th. anbede
                                              I. at tilbidia hñ

32. 1:25, peperit
   C. Heo cende hyre frum-cennedan sunu
   L.   *gecende*   K. bekande
                                              Th. bekende

33. 4:8, ostendit
   C. se deofol ... *æt*-eowde him ... ricu   T. araugta
   R.   *æt*eawde
   L.   *ge-eaude*
   "Commutation principle"

34. 8:4, ostende
   C. æt-eowe þe þam sacerde   T. *giougi*
   R. æt-eaw   G. ataugi
   L. æd-eau

35. 25:32, separabit
   C. hé asyndrað hí hym betwynan
         gesceadiþ   T. zisceidit
         to-sceades
   Wyc. "he schal *departe* hem atwynne"

36. 19:15, cum impossuisset
   C. þa he him hys handa on *asette*   T. anasatzta
   R.   *setteon*   K. up gelecht
   L.   *gesette* him   Th. lede up
   Wyc. "whenne he hadde *putte to* hem hondis"

   Cf. Mark 3:17, imposuit eis nomina
   C. him naman *onsette*
   L.   *gesette*   G. gasatida
                                                ("hinsetzen")

"Meaning" of the Morpheme

The *on-* of *onsette* here is probably not a reduction of *ond-* but the preposition *on*. Consequently in the light of all correspondences I would read *gesette* as 'He *set on to* them names.'
Wyc. "he putte *to* hem names"

37. 18:33, oportuit
    C. hu ne *gebyrede* þé gemiltsian   Th. borde to
    Wyc. "behovede . . . thee"

38. 21:39, apprehensam
    C. Ða namon hig . . . hyne
    R.   *gegripon*   Th. begrepen

39. 21:34, appropinquasset
    C. Ða ðara weastma tid *ge-nealæhte*
    R.   *to-nealehte*
    "Commutation principle"

40. 5:1, ascendit
    C. he *astag* on þone munt   I. *gieck vpp* a fiallit
    R.   *astahg*
    L.   *gestag*
    Wyc. "went *up in to* an hill"

41. 9:1, ascendens
    C. Ða *astag* he on scyp
    R.   *astigende*
    L.   *gestag*   G. atsteigands
    Wyc. "goyng *up in to* a boot"

42. 7:25, descendit
    C. þa com þær ren
    R.   *astag* niþer
    L.   afdune *gefeall*   G. attidja dalaþ
    Literally, in L., and historically, 'fell *forth* off the hill'

43. 8:1, discedisset
    C. se haelend of þam munte nyþer-*astah*   T. arsteig
    R.   wæs *astigen* of   I. geik ofan af fiallino
    L.   of *gestah*   G. Dalaþ atgaggandin

The last four sets above clearly illustrate the abstract and single relationship expressed by the morpheme *ge-*. Corresponding with OE *ā-* and

OHG *ar-* (both reflexes of IE **ud*) and meaning 'forth, away' *only*, its goal must be supplied by its context: 'up' by the preposition "*on*," 'down' by the preposition "*of*," indicating not the goal but the point of departure ('he moved forward on'—'he moved forward down or off').

44. 25:18, abscondit
 C. and *behydde* hys hlafurdes feoh;
 R.   *ahydde*   K. vorhudde
 L.   *gehydde*   Th. behudde
 Note especially the inter-dialectal substitutions.

45. 19:2, secutae sunt
 C. 7 hym fyligden mycele mænegu
 R.   *gefylgdon*   K. navolgede
 L.   fylgende weron   Th. volgedan na
                                   I. fylgdi epter

46. 26:58, sequebatur
 C. Petrus hym fylide feorranne
        folgade
            gefylgede   K. na folgede
                                   Th. volgede na
                                   I. fylgdi epter
 Wyc. "suede him after"
 LG *na* is generally translated by NHG *nach*, but both are related to OHG *nāh* originally meaning, according to Brugmann, "*herangewendet*."

47. 19:29, possidebit
 C. hé onfehþ lean 7 hæfð ece lif;
 R.   *gesitteð*   T. bisizzent
                                  Th. besitten
 Intrans. vb. + *ge-* + acc. object

48. 25:34, possidete
 C. onfoð þrice
 R. *gesittað*   T. gisizzet
                                  K. besittet
                                  Th. besittet
 Wyc. "take gee in *posession*"
 In the two preceding sets we have a situation that appears frequently, i.e., a compounded *intransitive* verb with an accusative outer object.

"Meaning" of the Morpheme

Modern grammarians are inclined to say that the prefix makes the intransitive verb a transitive one. This is oversimplification that ignores the history of this phenomenon and obscures the role of the prefix. It is the accusative form that is the active marker here and indicates that the object has the full force of the action of the verb *directed on to* it. The prefix does the directing. Therefore here literally: 'sit on to it.' This is a survival of a very old IE construction.

Contrasting pair:

49. 18:18, alligaveritis
    C. swa hwylce swa gé *ge-bindað* ofer eorþan.   T. gibintet

    18:18, solueritis
    C. swa hwylce swa ge ofer eorþan *únbindaþ*   M. antbindit

'Zubindet, anbindet,' = 'bind up,' as opposed to 'entbindet' = 'unbind.' There is no question of time or completion involved here, merely two kinds of binding; therefore two different *lexical* units.

50. 6:26, respicite
    C. Be-healdað heofonan fuglas
    R. *geseoþ*   K. seet an
        Th. seet an
        G. insaihiþ
        ("hin-ansehen")

Intrans. vb. + *ge-* + acc. object: 'see *on to* the fowels.' Here again a verb of sense perception regarded as a verb of motion. This idiom has of course survived into modern times: "Seht *zu* dass er euch nicht erwischt," "Er sah es sich *an*"; "You see *to* the financial arrangements," "See *to* it that you go."

Cf. 18:10, uidete
C. warniað þ ge ne oferhogian
R. *beseah*
L. *geseas*   I. Siaet til

'See to (it).' Cf. Luther: *Sehet zu* dass. . . .

51. 12:26, stabit
    C. Hú mæg þonne hys rice standan
    L.   *gestonde*   K. besteyt
        Th. bestan

'Stand *on*,' i.e., 'continue to stand'

52. 4:5, statuit
   C. se deofol *asette* hine ofer þæs temples heahness
   L.   *gesette*

   Certainly not 'set him together' or 'set him with' over the high place of the temple but 'set him out' in the one instance and 'set him forth' in the other, both of which can be *translated* into NE 'set him up,' NHG 'setzte ihn *hin*'

53. 9:29, tetigit
   C. Ða *æt-hran* he hyra eagena   T. biruorta
   R.   *æt-hran*   Th. berorde
   L.   *gehrán*   G. attaitok
                                              ("anrühren")

   Luther: "rürete jre augen *an*"

54. 16:24, tollat
   C. gyf hwa wylle fyligean me ... nyme hys rode
   L.   *genyme*   Th. bore up
                                              I. taki a sig

55. 2:3, turbatus est
   C. ða wearð he *gedrefed*   K. bedrouet
   R.   *gedroefed*   Th. bedrouet
                  gedroefed
   Literally 'be-troubled'

Contrasting pair:
56. 27:31, induerunt
   C. hig ... scryddon hyne
   R.   *gegearwadun*   T. *giuuatitun*
   L.   *ge-geredon*   G. *gawasidona*
                                              ("bekleiden")
                                              11.8
                                          Th. deden an
                                          I. foerdu hñ aptri

57. 27:31, exuerunt
   C. hig unscryddon hyne
   R.   *ungeredun*   T. *intuuatitun*
   L.   *ongeredon*   G. *andwasidedun*
                                              ("entkleiden")
                                              Mark 15:20
                                          K. togen vth
                                          Th. toghen vth
                                          I. foerdu hñ vt

"Meaning" of the Morpheme 49

58. 9:4, uidisset
 C. þa se haelend *geseah* hyra ge-þanc
 R. *geseende* Th. sah an
 L. *gesæh*
 Intrans. vb. + *ge-* + acc. object; therefore 'saw *on to*,' not 'had seen'

59. 5:28, uiderit
 C. aelc þæra þe wif *gesyhð*
 R. *gesihþ* I. litr til
 L. *gesis*
 Here an excellent illustration of the difference between *seon* and *geseon*
 Luther: "ansieht"
 A.V. "looketh on"

60. 27:35, diuiserunt
 C. hig *to-dældon* hys reaf.
 R. *gedældun*
 L. *todældon* T. ziteilit (24:51)

61. 2:7, uocatis
 C. Herodes þa clypode ... ða tungol-witegan   M. zu sich besante
 R. *acægde*   T. *gihaloten*
     ("herbeirufen")
 L. *geceigde*   K. vor sik halen
     I. kalladi til sin
 Wyc. "clepid *to hym*"
 Again a great difference between simplex and *ge-* compound

Contrasting pair:

62. 27:60, aduoluit
 C. he *to-awylte* mycelne stan to hlide þaere byrgene
 R. *to-wælde*
 L. *gewælte* T. zuogiuualzta
 C. 'rolled *out to*'; R. 'rolled *to*'; L. 'rolled *forth*'
 Wyc. "he *walowid to* a grete stoon *at* the dore"

 Cf. 28:2, reuoluit
 C. drihtenes engel ... *awylte* ðone stan   T. aruualzta
 R. *awælede*
 L. *eft-awælte*
 'Rolled away'
 Wyc. "turnide avvey the stoon"
 Here in these two sets, if anywhere at all, is unquestionable evidence that
 ge- still had *lexical* meaning in OE.

Contrasting pair:
63. Luke 4:17, reuoluit
    C. swa he þa boc *unf*éold   T. inteta
                   *un*tynde   G. uslukands
                    *on*tynde

    Cf. Luke 4:20, plicuisset
    C. and þa he þa bóc befeold   T. biteta
    R.   *gifylled*   (G. has simplex:
                                         "faifalþ")

    L.   *gefeald*

II. Ge- corresponds to preverbs, prepositions, or adverbs that can be translated by morphemes meaning 'out,' 'forth,' or 'away':

64. 7:26, aedificauit
    C. þe *getimbrode* hys hus   I. vpp bygdi
    L.   *getimberde*   G. gatimrida
    R.   timbrad   ("erbauen")
    L.   atimbra (25:40)
    Either 'built out' or 'built up'

65. 13:6, aruerunt
    C. hig ... forscruncon   M. ardorretun
    R.   forwisnadun   T. furthorretun
    L.   *gescrúungon*   K. vordorden
    Wyc. "drieden vp"
    A.V. "withered away"

66. 21:8, caedebant
    C. Sume heowun þæra treowa bogas
    R.   sneddun
    L.   *geðurscon*   K. slogen aff
    Wyc. "kittiden ... of"

67. 4:21, procedens
    C. And þa he þanon eode
    R.   *for*þgangande   K. vort ginck
    L.   *gefoerde*   Th. gink vort
                                               I. giek fram leingra
                                                  burt

    Wyc. "goynge forth"
    Luther: "ging fürbass"

"Meaning" of the Morpheme

68. 18:26, ──
    C. þa astrehte se þeow hyne
    R. *forþ-fallende*
    L. *gefeoll*
    Wyc. "fallynge doun"

    Th. vil vor ene
    I. fiell fram

69. 7:23, discedite
    C. *Gewitað* fram me
    R. *gewitaþ*
    L. afirres

    T. aruuizet
    K. Gat af
    G. afleiþiþ ("weggehn")

Literally: 'go out, away, from me'
Wyc. "departe *awey*"

70. 9:24, recedite
    C. Gað heonun
    R. *gewitaþ*
    L. *gewoendas*

    T. gét hina
    K. gad vt
    G. afleiþiþ

Wyc. "Go ge *awey*"

71. 2:13, recessissent
    C. þa hi þa ferdon
    R. *gewitenæ*
    L. *gewoendon*
    Wyc. "gon *awey*"

    T. thanon fuoron
    I. iburt farner

72. 25:41, discedite
    C. *Gewitað* fram me
    R. *gewitaþ*
    'Go forth from me'
    Luther: "gehet hin"

    T. eruuizet
    I. farit burt

73. 22:7, succendit
    C. se cyning ... hyra burh *forbærnde*
    R.   *forbernde*
    L.   *gebarn*
    'Burned away,' i.e., NE 'burned down'

    M. forbrennita
    T. bibranta
    Th. uorbrande

74. 14:32, cessauit
    C. þa *geswac* se wind
    L.   *geblann*

    T. bilan
    Th. vor gink
    I. fyrdi

'The wind moved away,' *not* 'stopped'

75. 27:60, exciderat
　　C. ða he *aheow* on stane
　　R. 　　*ge-heu*　　　　　　　　　　　I. vt hoggua
　　'Hewed out'

76. 7:19, exciditur
　　C. sy hyt *forcorfen*　　　　　　　　T. abafurhóuuan
　　R. 　　*acorfen*　　　　　　　　　　Th. af houwen
　　L. 　　*gecearfes* [Literally 'cut out']　I. af hogguit
　　　　　　　　　　　　　　　　　　　　G. usmaitada
　　　　　　　　　　　　　　　　　　　　　　("ausschneiden")

　　Note substitutions in the OE dialects.
　　Wyc. "kitte *doun*"

77. 14:26, clamaverunt
　　C. hi ... for þam ege clypodon
　　L. 　　　　　　*ge-clioppadon*
　　　　　　　　　　　　　　　　　　　　M. erscriun
　　　　　　　　　　　　　　　　　　　　T. arriofun
　　　　　　　　　　　　　　　　　　　　I. kolladu vpp
　　'Cried out'

78. Cf. Luke 1:42, exclamauit
　　C. heo clypode micelre stéfne.　　　　G. ufwopida
　　　　　　　　　　　　　　　　　　　　　　("ausrufen")
　　R. 　　*gicegde*
　　L. 　　*ge-ceigde*
　　'Cried out'

79. 12:26, creuisset
　　C. þa seo wyrt weox
　　L. 　　　*gewóx*　　　　　　　　　　M. uph ar uuchs
　　　　　　　　　　　　　　　　　　　　I. spratt upp
　　C. 'when the plant grew,' but L. 'when the plant grew *out* (up)'

80. 27:35, crucifixerunt
　　C. hig hyne on rode *ahengon*
　　R. 　　　　　　　　*ahongon*
　　L. 　　　　　　　　*gehengon*　　　　T. erhiengun
　　'Hung out'

81. 23:5, dilatant
　　C. Hig *to-brædað* hyra hals-bæc
　　L. 　　*gebrædas*　　　　　　　　　I. blaud vt
　　Wyc. "thei drawen *abrood* her filateries"
　　'Spread out'

"Meaning" of the Morpheme 53

82. 7:13, ducit
    C. se weg is swiþe rum þe to forspilledness *gelæt*   K. dar leydet
                                                          Th. dar geit
    Not 'leads' but 'leads away'
    Luther: "abführt"

83. 27:31, duxerunt
    C. hig ... læddon hyne to ahonne;
    R.   læddun
    L.   *gelæddon*
                                                          K. vorden ene vth
                                                          Th. ledden ene uth
                                                          I. leiddu hñ vt
    In C. and R. "konstatierend," in L. "schildernd." Here again the choice of simplex or compound lay with the writer. L. is generally more concrete and descriptive.
    Luther: "führten ihn hin"
    A.V. "led him away"

84. 27:2, adduxerunt
    C. hig læddon hyne gebundenne
    R.   læddun
    L.   *gelædon*
                                                          I. leiddu i burt
                                                          G. gatauhan
                                                             ("wegführen")
    'Led him forth, or away'
    Luther: "führeten ihn hin"
    A.V. "led him away"

85. 9:15, auferetur
    C. se bryd-guma byð afyrred
    R.   afirred
    L.   *genummen*
                                                          Th. benamen
                                                          G. afnimada

86. 20:3, egressus
    C. þa he út-eode embe undern-tide
    R.   út-eode
    L.   *gefoerde*
                                                          T. uzgangenti
                                                          K. uth gink
                                                          Th. gink ut
                                                          I. gieck vt

    Wyc. "gon *out*"

87. 22:10, egressi
    C. Ða eodon þa þeowas út
    R.   utgangende
    L.   *gefoerdon*
                                   M. fuorun uz
                                   T. gincgun uz
                                   K. ginghen ut
                                  Th. ginghen en wech
                                   I. geingu vt

    Wyc. "gon *out*"

88. 24:39, progressus
    C. þa he was ... þanon *agán*
    R.   *forþon gangende*
    L.   *gefoerde*
                                   T. ergieng
                                   K. gink vort
                                   I. gieck fram

    Wyc. "And he gon *forth* a litil"
    I doubt that *forþon* in R. means 'forthwith' as J. R. Clark Hall would have it; I believe that it means literally 'forth on,' and translates the *pro-* in *progressus*.

89. 20:24, indignati
    C. ða tyn leorning-cnihtas *gebulgon*   M. arbolgan
    R.   *abulgenne weron*
    Literally: 'they swelled out'

90. 7:5, eicere
    C. ꝥ þu ut-adó ꝥ mot
    R.   *awearpe*
    L.   *geworpe*
                                   T. aruuerphanne
                                   K. vth werpen
                                   I. vt dregit

    Wyc. "cast *out*"

91. 8:12, eicientur
    C. þisses rices bearn beoþ aworpene   T. foruuorphen
    R.   *aworpenne*   Th. vth worpen
    L.   *gedrifen*   I. vt reckner
                                                        G. uswairpanda

    Wyc. "cast *out*"

"Meaning" of the Morpheme 55

92. 19:22, abiit
    C. þa *eode* he *aweg* unrót   K. gink hen
    R.   *eode*   *aweg*   Th. gink en wech
    L.   *ge-eade*   I. gieck i burt
    Wyc. "he wente *awey*"
    A. V. "went away"

93. 18:30, ———
    C. He þa ... ferde 7 wearp hyne on cweartern.
    R.   eode
    L.   *ge-eade*   Th. gink en wech
                                       I. for til
    In such a context NLG can use either *güng hen* or, like Icelandic above, *güng to*.
    Wyc. "wente *out*"
    Luther: "ging hin"

94. 4:24, ———
    C. ða ferde his hlisa into ealle syriam
    R.   eode
    L.   *ge-eade*
                                       T. argieng
                                       K. uth ginck
                                       I. fylgdi epter vt

95. 22:22, abierunt
    C. [hig] *ferdon onweg*   M. kengun danan
    R.   *eodon awæg*   K. ginghen en wech
    L.   *ge-eadon*   Th. ginghen en wech
                                       I. geingu i burt

    Wyc. "they wenten *awey*"

96. 22:5, ———
    C. hig ... ferdun
    R.   *eodun aweg*
    L.   *gie-eadon*   Th. gingen en wech
                                       I. geingu i burt

    Wyc. "they wenten *awey*"
    Luther: "giengen hin"

97. 2:9, ———
    C. þa ferdon hig
    R.   *eoden þanon*   K. ginghen en wech
    L.   *geeadon*   Th. ginghen en wech
                                       I. foru afstad

Wyc. "wenten *awey*"

In the set immediately above R. and I. stress the point of departure, while K., Th., and L. stress the motion forward; the logical "sense" of all, however, is the same.

98. 13:3, exiit
    C. *ut-eode* se sǽdere hys saed to sawenne
    R. *ut eode*
    L. *ge-eade*
                                     M. fuor uz
                                       T. gieng thó úz
                                     Th. gink vth
                                       I. giek vth

    Wyc. "goth *out*"
    Luther: "gieng aus"

99. 12:43, ———
    C. þonne se unclaena gast *utfærþ*   M. uz argengit
    R.   *út gæþ*   T. úzǵet
    L.   *geeade*   Th. geit vth
                                              K. vth gink

    Wyc. "shal go *out*"

100. 9:26, ———
    C. þes hlisa sprang ofer eall ꝥ land
    R.   *eode*
    L.   *ge-eade*
                                         T. argieng
                                         K. gink vth
                                       Th. quemen vth
                                       I. barst vt
                                       G. usiddja

    Wyc. "And this fame wente *out*"

Note the following *contrast*:
101. 22:15, Tunc *abeuntes* pharisaei consilium *inierunt*
    L.   *ge-eadon*   *in-eoden*
    Wyc. "goynge *awey*"

102. 5:18, praeteribit
    C. án i oððe án prica ne *gewit* fram þære ǽ.   T. furferit
    R.   *gelioreþ*   K. vorgan
                                                         Th. vorgeit
                                                         I. foregang
                                                         G. usleiþiþ

    'Will not go *away*'

"Meaning" of the Morpheme 57

103. 24:34, ———
    C. ðeos cneorys ne *gewit*
    R.   *geleoraþ*

    M. zaferit
    K. vorgeit
    Th. schal nicht
         vorgan
    I. mun eigi
       forganga

104. 5:18, transeat
    C. ærþam *gewite* heofon 7 eorðe
    R.   *geleoreþ*

    T. zifare
    K. vergeit
    Th. vorgan
    I. forgeingr
    G. usleiþiþ

105. 12:18, elegi
    C. Her is mín cnapa þone ic *ge-ceas*
    R.   *geceas*
    L.   *geceas*
    'Chose out'

    K. vth vorkaren
    Th. vt vorkaren
    I. vt walda

106. 13:48, elegerunt
    C. þa *gecuron* hig þa godan
    R.   *gecuron*
    L.   *gecuron*

    M. aruuelitun
    T. arlasun
    K. lesen se uth
    Th. leset uth

107. 22:14, electi
    C. manega synt gelaþode 7 feawa *gecorene*
    R.   *gecorænæ*
    L.   *gecoreno*

    M. aruuelite
    K. vterkaren
    Th. vterkoren
    I. vtvalder

In the light of these correspondences above there is no reason to assume that *ge-* in the past participle is any different semantically from the others.

108. 12:11, leuabit
    C. he ... hefþ hytt upp
    R.   *ahefeþ*
    L.   *gehebbes*

    M. heuit uz
    T. ufheue
    K. havet up
    Th. uth bore
    I. vpp dregr

Wyc. "lift it vp"

Note that there is no conflict here between OHG *uz* and *uf*. We know that in Gothic, and consequently probably in Proto-Germanic, the reflex of IE **upo* could mean 'auf, unter, an, über-hin, aus.' Cf. Brugmann, *Grundriss*, p. 911; Kuhn, "Das Füllwort *of-* ...," p. 97.

109. 6:13, libera
    C. ac *alys* us of yfele   T. arlosi
    R. *gelese*   K. vorlose
         I. fyrelat

'Loose us *out* of evil'

110. 14:4, licet
    C. nys þe alyfed hí to wife to haebbenne   T. arlaubit
    R.   alefed
    L.   *gelefed*

111. 22:7, missis exercitibus
    C. he ... *sende* hys here *to* 7 fordyde þa manslagan
    L.   *gesendeno*   I. sendi vt

The *to* here in C. is used precisely as it can be in NLG, where it often means 'forth, ahead.'

112. 12:17, adimpleretur
    C. þ wære *gefylled* þ þe gecweden wæs   M. arfullit
    R.   *gefylled*   T. gifullit
    L.   *gefylled*   K. voruullet
         Th. voruullet

113. 28:9, impletum est
    C. Ða wæs *gefylled* þ gecweden is   M. arfullit
    R.   *gefyllad*   K. voruult
    L.   *gefylled*   Th. voruullet
         I. vppfyllt
         G. usfullnoda

There is ample evidence here that it is dangerous to assume that *ge-* even in the past participle is an empty morpheme that has become "grammaticized" and consequently is without meaning. Here literally 'filled out'

114. 2:16, exquisierat
    C. þe he *ge-axode* fram ðam tungol-witegum
    R.   *a*sohte
    L.   *gesohte ł gefragade*   K. hadde vornamen
         I. vt spurt

"Meaning" of the Morpheme

Wyc. "that he hadde *sougt out* of the kyngis."
Not "gained by asking" but 'asked out.' (This is a *ge-* of achievement.) Exactly like its Latin counterpart, once univerbalized *geacsian* can mean 'find out.'

115. 5:29, erue
    C. ahola hit út
    R. ahloca
    L. *gener ɫ genim* [not followed by *ut*]

    T. árlosi
    K. brick dat vth
    Th. brik it vth
    I. kipp þui vt
    G. usstag ("stich aus")

Luther: "reiss es aus"
A.V. "pluck it out"

116. 23:34, persequimini
    C. ge hig *ehtað* of byrig on byrig
    R.   *oehtaþ*
    L.   *ge-oehtas*

    Vienna fragment: ir ahtet ir us
    I. of soekia
    K. voruolget (5:12)

Literally: 'you judge them out,' i.e., '*out*law them'

117. 12:13, extende
    C. *aþene* þine hand
    R. *aþene*
    L. *geðen*

    T. artheni
    K. strekke vth
    Th. Do hir vore
    I. viett vt

Wyc. "Streeche *forth* thin hond"
Luther: "Strecke deine hand *aus*"
A.V. "Stretch *forth* thine hand"

118. 8:3, extendens
    C. Ða astrehte se hælend hys hand
    R.   aþenede
    L.   *gespræde*

    T. utstreckede
    Th. reckede uth
    I. vt rietti
    G. ufrakjands ("ausstrecken")

Wyc. "holdynge *forthe* the hand"

Contrasting sets:

119. 13:44, uendit
    C. [se man] sylþ eall þ he ah
    R.   *bebygið*   T. furcoufit
    L.   *bebyges*   K. vorkofft
                                                  Th. vorkopet

    13:46, uendidit
    R. he ... sealde eall þ he ahte   M. forchaufta
    L.   *bobohte*   T. furcoufta
    'Sold,' but:

    27:7, emerunt
    C. þa *gebohton* hig ænne æcyr   M. gachaufit (13:44)
    R.   *gebohton*   T. gachaufte
                                                      (13:46)
    L.   *gebohton*   G. usbauhtedun
                                                      ("erkauften")

The contrast above amply illustrates the futility of trying to explain *ge-* by saying that it "perfectivates." In their respective contexts above both *bebycgan* and *gebycgan* express a "perfective" *Aktionsart*; yet obviously the two prefixes *be-* and *ge-* delimit the verb semantically and create compounds each with a different meaning. Here, then, 'they bought *out* an acre'

120. 11:5, uident
    C. blinde *geseoþ*   G. ussaihand
    R.   *geseeþ*
    L.   *geseað*

    Cf. Mark 10:51, uideam
    C. hwæt wilt þu þ ic þe dó;
        þa cwæð he. lareow þ ic *geseo*   G. ussaihua
    L.   *gesii*

A verb of motion again, therefore I conjecture that the meaning was like that in Goth., since the verb is definitely intransitive here; therefore 'see out,' or 'see forth.' Cf. Fritz Bechtel, *Ueber die Bezeichnungen der sinnlichen Wahrnehmungen in den indogermanischen Sprachen* (Weimar, 1879): "... sehen fällt zusammen mit *scharf sein, durchdringen*. Das got. *saihuan* mit lat. *secare* gleiche basis habe weiss mann schon längst" (p. 160). A more likely cognate is Lat. *sequor*.

III. The Latin com- compounds (note that nowhere do com- and ge- correspond with any morpheme meaning 'zusammen' or 'mit'):

121. 22:10, congregauerunt
    C. þa þeowas *gegaderedon* ealle   K. vorgadderdon

"Meaning" of the Morpheme   61

122. 24:31, congregabunt
    C. hi *ge-gaderigað* hys gecorenan   Th. vorgaddert

123. 14:35, cum cognouissent
    C. þa ꝥ folc hyne *gecneow*   T. incantun
    L.   *oncneawon*   K. bekanden
                  Th. bekenden

124. 21:10, commota
    C. þa wearð eall seo burh-waru *onstyred*   K. beweghet
    L.   *gestyred*   Th. beweghen

125. 6:29, coopertus
    C. salomon ... næs *ofer-wrigen*   T. bithekkit
    L.   *gegearued*   K. bedecket
                  G. gawosida
                    ("bekleidet")

126. 4:24, comprehensos
    C. on tintregum *gegripene*   T. bifangane
    R.   *gefongnæ*   K. bevanghen
    L.   *begetna*   Th. begrepen

127. 6:28, considerate
    C. Besceawiað æcyres lilian
    R. *gesceawigaþ*   Th. seet an
                  I. hyggit at
                  G. gakunniaþ
                  ("erkennen")

    'See on to'

128. 21:44, conteret
    C. he *to-brysð* þone ðe he onuppon fylð   T. zibrihhit
    R.   *gehnyscet*   K. to wrifft
    L.   *gebrecceð*   Th. to knadderen

129. 13:15, conuertantur
    C. þe læs hig ... sin *gecyrde*   K. bekert
    R.   *ge-cerrede*   Th. bekeren
    L.   *gecerre*

130. 9:22, conuersus
    C. se hælend bewende hyne
    R.   gecerde
    L.   gecerde

    K. kerde sik umme
    Th. kerde sic umme
    G. gawandjans sik
         ("hinwenden")

    'Turned himself to'

131. 7:6, conculcent
    C. þe læs hig ... hig *fortredon*
    R.   tredon
    L.   *getrede*

    T. furtreten
    K. vortreden
    Th. to treden

132. 5:13, conculcetur
    C. ꝥ hit ... sy fram mannum *for-treden*
    R.   tredan
    L.   *getreden*

    K. vortreden
    Th. to treden
    I. for trodit

133. 12:41, condemnabunt
    C. hig *genyþeriað* hig
    L.   *geniðras*

    T. furniderent

134. 13:28, colligimus
    C. wylt þu we gáð 7 gadriað hig
    R.   *gesomnige*

    T. arlesemes íz úz
    K. lesen se vth
    Th. vth lesen
    I. vt lesam

135. 13:40, colliguntur
    C. swa swa se coccel by þ *gegaderud*
                gesomnad
                gesomnad

    T. arlesen sint
    K. vorgaadert
    I. vt lesit

136. 11:1, cum consumasset
    C. þa se hælynd þys *ge-endude*
    L.   *gefylde*   G. usfullida
    Translated into NE idiom: 'When the Saviour ended this up' ("schildernd" rather than "konstatierend"), NHG 'beendete.'

IV

One could substantially increase the above list of relatively full sets of correspondences, for Matthew yielded 485 such sets, all about equally rich in correspondences. However, at this point it seems best to apply Ockham's razor.

"Meaning" of the Morpheme

What the above correspondences indicate is, I think, perfectly clear: *ge-* means precisely the same as Armenian *z*, "den Weg einer Bewegung," or, as I have stated it, "that the action of the verb to which it is affixed is directed forward *toward* something or *outward*." It expresses a relation which in the terms of logic has an asymmetrical sense: 1. (⊢→) transitive and *imperfective*, i.e., as Grimm had already observed, capable of indicating that an action continues on indefinitely, and 2. (⊢→|) intransitive and *perfective*, i.e., capable of expressing not a perfective *aspect*, but a perfective *Aktionsart*, as understood by the conventional linguists of the nineteenth and early twentieth centuries and as best expressed by Behaghel as an "Übergang aus einem Berührungszustand in ein Nichtberührungszustand" (see sets 65, 67, 69, 74, 77, 79, 84, 89, 102, 111, 120, where *ge-* has the contextual meaning of 'out, away') "oder das Umgekehrte" (see sets 2, 13, 26, 27, 36, 44, 50, 53, 56, where *ge-* has the contextual meaning of 'to, on, or *be-*'). Nowhere is there any evidence that *ge-* meant 'zusammen, mit, together'; rather the evidence indicates that the linguistic signs necessary to express the abstract relationship are the NE morphemes *to, on, onto, on to, forth, out* and *away*, at times even *up* and *down*, or the NHG morphemes *an, zu, aus, hinweg, hin*; "le valeur de n'importe quel terme est déterminée par ce qui l'entoure" (deSaussure, *Cours*, p. 167).

Consequently the evidence corroborates the empirical observations not of Streitberg but of Grimm, Pott, Goropius, Kuhn, and Heusler; it re-affirms the fact that the function of *ge-* is not syntactic but lexical; it removes Brugmann from the horns of his dilemma in that it reveals that the morpheme shows the same deixis as its phonological cognate IE **gho-*; and it explains why OE compounds in *ge-* translate Latin compounds in *ad-* as frequently as or more frequently than those in *com-*. Finally, it effects the reconciliation between perfectivation and lexical meaning that Wustmann demanded.

That *ge-* must be translated by means of a variety of NE morphemes is inherent in the very abstract nature of preverbs and even in the nature of prepositions—and it is normal. (Bosworth-Toller give fifteen different meanings for the preverb *be-* and twelve even for the preposition *aet*). That it meant 'out' is confirmed by the operation of the commutation principle in the OE versions of Matthew, where on the basis of a strict lexical count Lindisfarne translates Latin compounds in *ex-* with twenty *different* and separate compounds in *ge-* whereas Rushworth and Corpus translate them with compounds in *a-*; that it also meant 'to' is confirmed by evidence as early as the OHG glosses:

p. 44, 38,	Adheserunt:	*az* clepeton	*az* klipun	kachlipun
p. 124, 32,	deiudicatur:	*za*sonit	kisonit	
p. 154,3,	confusus:	*za*fleozzant:	*zi*fleozzendi	kifleozanti
p. 261,1,	Tumida:	*zi*suuollan	kisuollen	
p. 46, 1,	Aduerte:	kahuuerue	kiuuerui	*zo* uuerpi

p. 188, 29, quod *adire* non potest:
>daz *za*cangan ni mac   thar man *kikankan* ni mac[47]

The basic "sense" of both of these meanings can be expressed by NE *forth, to*.

The fact that in translating from Old English to modern English *ge-* in its various contexts must be replaced by several different NE morphemes does not imply that in Old English *ge-* was polysemous; it is the exigencies of translation that make it seem so. Rather, it appears to have been monosemous, its sememe being simply the abstract meaning stated above. And this sememe appears to have been closely related to the sememe of the morpheme *to-*, especially where the latter appeared as a preverb in other Germanic dialects, as it still does in the NLG dialect of Scheswig-Holstein and the Lüneburg Heath.

In fact, only on the analogy with the idiom in this dialect can one possibly clarify two glosses in Lindisfarne Matt. 25:5:

> *ge*slepeden alle 7 *ge*slepdon
> dormitaverunt omnes et dormierunt

The sense here is obviously 'they fell asleep and they continued sleeping,' but the second gloss plays havoc with the followers of Streitberg who insist that *ge-* compounds are punctual only, and it prompted Weick to reject the reading on the grounds of textual corruption. But NLG has an exact semantic parallel to these two OE compounds if these are interpreted in the light of the meaning of *ge-* adduced above, namely *tóslapen*:

> "Un daröwer *slapt* se weder *to*" ('and on that they *fall asleep* again')
> "... un so *slapt* se beid bet morgens *to*" ('and so the two *continue to sleep* until dawn')[48]

It is situations like this that break down the hypothesis of Streitberg; on the other hand they obviously corroborate the views of Jacob Grimm.

What is not always easy is determining which of the possible NE morphemes available will in translating produce a correct "idiomatic" rendering of the OE idiom; for the *precise* OE idiom, the expression of the manner in which an Anglo-Saxon thought, is not always clear. Especially is this the case when an OE *ge-* compound had become univerbalized and consequently no longer meant literally the sum of its immediate constituents. Moreover, the modern translator is often too prone to project his manner of thinking into the structural mass of the older language and is too reluctant to admit that its arrangement of *ideas* might be different from his own. Consequently, such a passage as Matt. 7:3, "þu ne *ge-syhst* þone beam" he hesitates to translate as 'thou dost not see *to* that beam' just as he hesitates to translate the intransi-

---

[47] *Die althochdeutschen Glossen*, ed. Elias Steinmeyer and Eduard Sievers (Berlin, 1879), 1.
[48] *Plattdeutsche Volksmärchen*, ed. Wilhelm Wisser (Jena, 1919), pp. 137, 148.

tive Matt. 11:5, "blinde *geseoþ*" with 'the blind see *forth*' or 'see out.' Such reluctance will also cause him to miss the finer nuances that the preverb produced in instances where it functioned in the manner that Sievers called "schildernd" and will prompt him to overlook the fact that *Beowulf* 2100, "meregrund *gefeoll*" is not to be translated by 'he gained the bottom of the mere by falling' but simply by 'he fell *on to* (down to) the bottom of the mere' (a very old IE accusative construction). Likewise he would fail to see that Alfred's *Orosius* 17, 20 "þa *siglde* he þanon suþryhte be londe swa swa he mehte on fif dagum *gesiglan*" has to be translated 'Then he sailed from that place straight south along the land as far as he was able to *sail out* (to) in five days,' or, as recast into NHG, using *hin* (phonologically cognate with Lat. *com-*) '... so weit wie er in fünf Tagen *hin* segeln konnte.' Such is the simple and obvious explanation of the appearance of both simplex and *ge-* compound in one and the same utterance—not the assumption that such simultaneous appearance bears witness to the fact that the Anglo-Saxon writer had lost all sense of the meaning of *ge-* and consequently interchanged the use of simplex and compound synonymously, capriciously, and indifferently, as many grammarians have tried to make us believe when they attempted to account for the ultimate loss of the morpheme.

The loss of the morpheme was due not to phonological weakening, as Herbert Pilch suggests,[49] but probably to the fact that during the Middle English period the whole OE preverbal *system* broke down and was supplanted by verb-adverb, verb-preposition combinations, as Mossé pointed out long ago.[50]

Far from being an "empty morpheme," *ge-* was replete with shades of meaning roughly equivalent to the NE morphemes *to* and *out*, and we can no longer rest upon the idle assumption that, because they appear to make no distinctive sense to us, such pairs as *seon-geseon* or *sittan-gesittan* appear in our texts as pseudosynonyms produced by indifference or sheer caprice. Not at all; each word is a separate and distinct lexical unit.

Whether or not the precise lexical meaning of OE *ge-* was still alive in the conscious reflections of the average speaker of Late Old English poses a question that can not be answered with certainty here; it falls beyond the scope of this work, which is interested solely in the *original* meaning of the morpheme at whatever time in the history of the language it was most productive. In the light of all of the evidence I am inclined to say yes, it was. If it was not, it doubtless had the same lexical status as NHG *ver-*. The average speaker of NHG is certainly not aware of the fact that *ver-* represents a fusion of several OHG preverbs that could mean 'before, forward, onto' and 'forth'; yet *ver-*

---

[49] Herbert Pilch, "Der Untergang des Präverbs *ge-* im Englischen," *Anglia*, LXXIII, 1 (1955), especially pp. 38–49.
[50] Mossé, *Histoire*, II, 23–26.

continues to be productive and contributes to the lexical contrasts between such words as *sehen*, *besehen*, *ersehen*, and *versehen*. And just as the capacity to handle such a compound effectively is the mark of an educated speaker of modern German, so no doubt was the proper handling of distinctions between *ge-* compounds and other compounds, or simplexes, one of the marks of the educated and linguistically proficient Anglo-Saxon.

Works Consulted

Aelfrics Grammatik und Glossar, ed. Julius Zupitza. Berlin, 1880.
Ahlman, Erik. *Über das lateinische Präfix* com- *in Verbalzusammensetzungen*. Helsingfors, 1916.
Anderson, George K. *The Literature of the Anglo-Saxons*. Princeton, 1949.
Bartholomae, Chr. "Beiträge zur Etymologie der germanischen Sprachen," *ZfdW*, IX (1907), 18-20.
Beer, Antonin. "Beiträge zur gotischen Grammatik," *PBB*, XLIII (1918), 446-69.
Behaghel, Otto. *Deutsche Syntax*, II. Heidelberg, 1924.
——. *Heliand und Genesis*. Halle/Saale, 1933.
Berner, Nils, *Die mit der Partikel* ge- *Gebildeten Wörter im Heliand*. Lund, 1900.
Bernhardt, E. "*Ga-* als Hilfsmittel bei der gotischen Conjugation," *ZfdPh*, II (1870), 158-66.
The Holy Bible, Authorized Version. Oxford, n.d.
Blain, H. M. *Syntax of the Verb in the A-S Chronicle*. New York, 1901.
Bloomfield, Leonard. *Language*. New York, 1933.
——. "Notes on the Preverb *ge-* in Alfredian English," in *Studies in English Philology: A Miscellany in Honor of Frederick Klaeber*, ed. Kemp Malone and Martin B. Ruud. Minneapolis, 1929.
Bonfante, G. "Notes sur l'histoire du verbe *venio*," *L'Antiquité Classique*, VIII (1939), 15-20.
Bréal, M. "Etymologies grecques et latines," *Mém. Soc. Ling.*, XV (1908-09), 341-43.
Brøndal, Viggo. *Théorie des prépositions*. Trans. Pierre Naert. Copenhagen, 1950.
Brugmann, Karl. *Kurze vergleichende Grammatik der indogermanischen Sprachen*. Berlin and Leipzig, 1933.
——. "Zu den reduplizierten Verbalbildungen des Indoiranischen," *IF*, XXXI (1912-13), 89-105.
Brugmann, Karl, und Berthold Delbrück. *Grundriss der vergleichenden Grammatik der indogermanischen Sprachen*. 2nd ed. Strassburg, 1897-1916.
Brusendorff, Aage. "The Relative Aspect of the Verb in English," in *Grammatical Miscellany Offered to Otto Jespersen on His Seventieth Birthday*. London, 1930. Pp. 56-88.
Buck, C. D. *A Grammar of Oscan and Umbrian*. Boston, 1904.
Bugge, Sophus. "Etymologische Studien über germanische Lautverschiebung," *PBB*, XII (1887), 399-431.
Caro, G. "Das englische Perfectum und Praeteritum in Ihrem Verhältnis zu einander historisch untersucht," *Anglia*, XXI (1899), 56-89.
Chadwick, D. E., C. B. Judge, A. S. C. Ross. "Collation of an Extract from the Lindisfarne Gospels, "*Leeds Studies*, No. 3 (1934).
Curme, Geo. O. "The Development of Verbal Compounds in Germanic," *PBB*, XXXIX (1914), 320-61.

_____. *A Grammar of the English Language.* Vols. II and III. Boston, n.d.
Curtius, Georg. *Grundzüge der griechischen Etymologie.* Leipzig, 1819.
Dahm, Karl. *Der Gebrauch von gi- zur Unterscheidung perfektiver und imperfektiver Aktionsart im Tatian und in Notkers Boethius.* Leipzig, 1909.
Delbrück, Berthold. *Vergleichende Syntax der indogermanischen Sprachen.* Vols. I and II. Strassburg, 1900.
Dorfeld, K. *Über die Function des Präfixes ge- (got. ga-) in der Composition mit Verben,* Teil 1: *Das Präfix bei Ulfilas und Tatian.* Giessen, 1885.
Drake, A. *The Authorship of the West Saxon Gospels.* New York, 1894.
Eckhardt, Eduard. *Das Präfix Ge- in verbalen Zusammensetzungen bei Berthold von Regensburg.* Leipzig, 1889.
Friedrichsen, G. W. S. *The Gothic Version of the Gospels.* London, 1926.
Gamillscheg, E. *Französische Bedeutungslehre.* Tübingen, 1951.
Giles, P. *Short Manual of Comparative Philology for the Use of Classical Students.* London and New York, 1901.
Gluntz, H. *Die lateinische Vorlage der westsächsischen Evangelienversion in seinem Verhältnis zur irisch-angelsächsischen Kultur des Frühmittelalters.* Leipzig, 1928.
Goedsche, C. R. "Aspekt versus Aktionsart," *JEGP,* XXXIX (1940), 122-28.
_____. "The Terminate Aspect of the Expanded Form," *JEGP,* XXXI (1932), 469-77.
_____. "Verbal Aspect in German," *JEGP,* XXXIII (1934), 506-19.
Grassmann, H. "Ursprung der Präpositionen im Indogermanischen," *KZ,* XXIII (1877), 550-80.
Gray, Louis H. *Foundations of Language.* New York, 1939.
Grimm, Jacob. *Deutsche Grammatik.* 2nd ed., rev. by Scherer. Berlin, 1878.
Hahn, E. Adelaide. "The Origin of the Relative *Kwi-Kwo-,*" *Language,* XXII (1946), 69-85.
Handke, R. *Über das Verhältnis der westsächsischen Evangelienübersetzung zum lateinischen Original.* Halle, 1896.
Harris, L. M. *Studies in the Anglo-Saxon Version of the Gospels.* Baltimore, 1891.
Hendrikson, J. R. "Old English Prepositional Compounds in Relationship to Their Latin Originals," *Language Dissertation No. 43,* Linguistic Society of America. Philadelphia, 1948.
Herbig, Gustav. "Aktionsart und Zeitstufe," *IF,* VI (1896), 157-269.
Hermann, Ed. "Aspekt und Aktionsart," *Nachrichten der Gesellschaft der Wissenschaften zu Göttingen,* Philologisch-Historische Klasse aus dem Jahre 1933, pp. 470-80.
_____. "Objektive und subjektive Aktionsart," *IF,* XLV (1927), 207-28.
Hesse, Hugo. *Perfektive und imperfektive Aktionsart im Altenglischen.* Münster i. Westfalen, 1906.
Hickes, George. *Institutiones Grammaticae.* Oxford, 1689.
Hirt, Hermann. *Etymologie der neuhochdeutschen Sprache.* Muenchen, 1909.
_____. *Handbuch des Urgermanischen.* Vols. II and III. Heidelberg, 1932, 1934.
_____. *Indogermanische Grammatik.* Vols. III, IV, VI, VII. Heidelberg, 1927-37.
Hollmann, Else. *Untersuchungen über Aspekt und Aktionsart unter besonderer Berücksichtigung des Altenglischen.* Teildruck. Würzburg, 1937.
Holthausen, F. *Altsächsisches Elementarbuch.* Heidelberg, 1900.
Hoops, Johannes. *Kommentar zum Beowulf.* Heidelberg, 1932.

Works Consulted

Hubbard, Frank G. "Beowulf 1598, 1996, 2026; Uses of the Impersonal Verb *geweorþan*," *JEGP*, XVII (1918), 119-25.
Jespersen, Otto. *A Modern English Grammar on Historical Principles*. Heidelberg, 1909.
———. *The Philosophy of Grammar*. New York, 1924.
Joly, André. "*Ge-* prefixe lexical en vieil anglais," *Canadian Journal of Linguistics*, XII (1967), 78-89.
Klaeber, Fr. "The Functions of Old English *geweorðan*," *JEGP*, XVIII (1919), 250-72.
———. "Semasiological Notes," *Modern Philology*, III (1905-6), 260-64.
———. "Zur altenglischen Bedeutungslehre," *Archiv für das Studium der neueren Sprachen und Literaturen*, CIX (1902), 309-14.
Kluge, F. "Sprachhistorische Miscellen," *PBB*, VIII (1882), 533-35.
———. *Urgermanisch*. 3d. ed. Strassburg, 1913.
Kock, Ernst A. "Interpretations and Emendations of Early English Texts," *Anglia*, XLII, Neue Folge XXX (1918), 99-125.
Koschmieder, E. "Studien zum slavischen Verbalaspekt," *KZ*, LV (1928), 280-305; LVI (1928), 78-105.
———. "Zu den Grundfragen der Aspekttheorie," *IF*, LIII (1935), 280-300.
Krömer, Gotthard. "Die Präpositionen in der hochdeutschen Genesis und Exodus," *PBB*, XXXIX (1914), 402-503.
Kruisinga, E. *A Handbook of Present-Day English*. Part 2. 5th ed. Groningen, 1931-32.
Lawson, Richard H. "A Reappraisal of the Function of the Prefix *gi-* in the Old High German *Tatian*," *Neuphilologische Mitteilungen*, LXIX (1968), 272-80.
Lehmann, Wilhelm. *Das Präfix uz- Besonders im Altenglischen*. Kiel, 1906.
Lenz, P. *Der syntaktische Gebrauch der Partikel "ge" in den Werken Alfreds des Grossen*. Darmstadt, 1886.
Lorz, Ant. *Aktionsarten des Verbums in Beowulf*. Würzburg, 1908.
Luick, K. *Historische Grammatik der englischen Sprache*. Leipzig, 1921-29.
Luther, Martin. *Die deutsche Bibel*, VI. Weimar, 1929. (This is vol. LXIV of *D. Martin Luthers Werke*. In this study I have used the 1546 text of *Matthew* collated with that of 1522.)
Maier, Gustav. "Das *ge-* Partizip im Neuhochdeutschen," *ZfdW*, I, Heft 4, 281-318.
Makovskij, M. M. "K probleme vida v gotskam jazyke," *Ucenye Zapiski*, XIX (Moscow, 1959), 41-99.
Martens, Heinrich. "Die verba perfecta in der Nibelungendichtung," *KZ*, XII (1863), 31-41, 321-35.
Meillet, A. "Étymologies slaves," *Mém. Soc. Ling.*, IX (1896), 49-55.
———. *Linguistique historique et linguistique génerale*. Paris, 1948.
———. "Notes sur quelque faits gothique," *Mém. Soc. Ling.*, XV (1908-9), 73-104.
Mourek, V. E. A review of Wustmann, in *ZfdA, Anzeiger* XXI (1895), 195 ff.
Paul, Hermann. *Mittelhochdeutsche Grammatik*. 15th ed. Halle/Saale, 1950.
Pedersen, Holger. "Zur Lehre von den Aktionsarten," *KZ*, XXXVII (1904), 219-50.
Pietsch, P. "Einige Bemerkungen ueber *ge-* bei Verben," *PBB*, XIII (1889), 516-30.
Pilch, Herbert. "Das AE. Präverb *ge-*," *Anglia*, LXXI, 2 (1953), 129-40.
———. "Der Untergang des Präverbs *ge-* im Englischen." Unpublished diss. in typescript (Christian Albrecht Universität). Kiel, 1951.
Pollak, H. W. "Studien zum germanischen Verbum," *PBB*, XLIV (1920), 353-426.

Pott, A. F. *Etymologische Forschungen auf dem Gebiete der indogermanischen Sprachen.* Lemgo and Detmold, 1859.
Poutsma, H. *The Characters of the English Verb.* Groningen, 1921.
Prokosch, Eduard. *A Comparative Germanic Grammar.* (William Dwight Whitney Linguistic Series). Philadelphia, 1939.
Raith, Joseph. *Untersuchungen zum englischen Aspekt.* 1. Teil: *Grundsätzliches, Altenglisch.* München, 1951.
Recha, Carl. *Zur Frage über den Ursprung der perfectivierenden Function der Verbalpräfixe.* Dorpat, 1893.
Reifferscheid, Al. "Lexicalisch-Syntaktische Untersuchungen über die Partikel *ge-,*" *Z fdPh,* Ergänzungsband (1874), pp. 319-446.
Rice, Alan L. "Gothic Prepositional Compounds in Their Relation to Their Greek Originals," *Language Dissertation No. 11,* Linguistic Society of America. Philadelphia, 1932.
Roedder, E. C. "Gothic *gasaihwan*: A Study in Germanic Synonyms," *PMLA,* LII (1937), 613-24.
Rosen, Harold. "Old High German Prepositional Compounds, in Relation to Their Latin Originals," *Language Dissertation No. 16,* Linguistic Society of America. Philadelphia, 1934.
Ross, A. S. C. "The Errors in the Old English Gloss to the Lindisfarne Gospels," *Review of English Studies,* VIII (1932), 385-95.
———. *Studies in the Accidence of the Lindisfarne Gospels.* Leeds School of English Language Texts and Monographs: No. II. Leeds, 1937.
Samuels, M. L. "The *ge-* Prefix in the Old English Gloss to the Lindisfarne Gospels," *Transactions of the Philological Society.* London, 1949. Pp. 62-114.
Santesson, Carl G. *La particule* cum *comme préposition dans les langues romanes.* Paris, 1921.
Senn, A. "Verbal Aspects in Germanic, Slavic, and Baltic," *Language,* XXV (1949), 402-9.
Shipley, George. *The Genitive Case in Anglo-Saxon Poetry.* Baltimore, 1903.
Sievers, Eduard. *Angelsächsische Grammatik,* revised by Karl Brunner under the title *Altenglische Grammatik.* 2nd ed. Halle/Saale, 1951.
Skeat, Walter W. *The Gospel According to Saint Matthew in Anglo-Saxon, Northumbrian, and Old Mercian Versions, Synoptically Arranged, with Collations Exhibiting All the Readings of All the MSS.* Cambridge, 1887.
Steinmeyer, Elias and Eduard Sievers. *Die althochdeutschen Glossen.* Vols. I, II. Berlin, 1879.
Streitberg, Wilhelm. *Die gotische Bibel.* 2nd ed. Erster Teil, Heidelberg, 1919; Zweiter Teil, Heidelberg, 1928.
———. "Perfective und imperfective actionsart im Germanischen," *PBB,* XV (1891), 70-178.
———. *Urgermanische Grammatik,* ("Unveränderter Abdruck der 1. Auflage (1896)"). Heidelberg, 1943.
———. A review of Wustmann, in *IF,* V (1895), *Anzeiger,* 78-83.
Thurneysen, Rudolph. *A Grammar of Old Irish.* Trans. D. A. Binchy and Osborn Bergin. Dublin, 1946.
———. *Handbuch des Alt-Irischen.* Heidelberg, 1909.

Tobler, L. "Über die Bedeutung des deutschen ge- vor Verben," *KZ*, XIV (1864), 108-39.
Trnka, B. "Some Remarks on the Perfective and Imperfective Aspects in Gothic," *Dona Natalicium Schrijnen* (Nijmegen-Utrecht, n.d., 1929?), pp. 496-500.
Van Draat, P. Fijn. "The Loss of the Prefix *Ge-* in the Modern English Verb and Some of Its Consequences," *Englische Studien*, XXXI, 3 (1906), 353-84.
Van Helten, W. L. *Die altostniederfränkischen Psalmenfragmente*. Groningen, 1902.
Van Swaay, H. A. J. *Het prefix ga- gi- ge-, zijn geschiednis, en zijn invloed op de "Actionsart" meer bijzonder in het Oudnederfrankisch en het Oudsaksisch*. Utrecht, 1901.
Vendryes, J. *Language*. Trans. Paul Eadin. New York, 1951.
Wadstein, Elis. "Die Entwicklung von urnord. *ga- w-*," *Beiträge zur Kunde der indogermanischen Sprachen*, XXII (1897), 114-18.
———. "Nordische Bildungen mit dem Präfix *ga-*," *IF*, V (1895), 1-32.
Weick, Friedrich. *Das Aussterben des Präfixes* ge- *im Englischen*. Darmstadt, 1911.
Wilmanns, W. *Deutsche Grammatick, Gotisch, Alt- Mittel-, und Neuhochdeutsch*. 3 vols: I, 3d ed. Strassburg, 1911; II, 2d ed. Berlin and Leipzig, 1922; III, 1, Berlin and Leipzig, 1922; III, 2, Strassburg, 1909.
Wisser, Wilhelm, ed. *Plattdeutsche Volksmärchen*. Jena, 1919.
Wright, Joseph. *Grammar of the Gothic Language*. Oxford, 1910.
———, and Elizabeth Mary Wright. *Old English Grammar*, 3d ed. Oxford, 1925.
Wustmann, Rudolf. *Verba Perfectiva namentlich im Heliand*. Leipzig, 1894.
Wuth, Alfred. *Aktionsarten der Verba bei Cynewulf*. Weida i. Thür. 1915.
Zeuss, I. C. *Grammatica Celtica*. 2nd ed. Berlin, 1871.